Mastering Linux - Servers

A catalogue record for this book is available from the Hong Kong Public Libraries.

Published in Hong Kong by Samurai Media Limited.

Email: info@samuraimedia.org

ISBN 978-988-8406-18-0

Background Cover Image by https://www.flickr.com/people/webtreatsetc/

Table of Contents

List of Tables

Part I. apache and squid

Table of Contents

Chapter 1. apache web server

In this chapter we learn how to setup a web server with the **apache** software.

According to NetCraft (http://news.netcraft.com/archives/web_server_survey.html) about seventy percent of all web servers are running on Apache. The name is derived from **a patchy** web server, because of all the patches people wrote for the NCSA httpd server.

Later chapters will expand this web server into a LAMP stack (Linux, Apache, Mysql, Perl/PHP/Python).

1.1. introduction to apache

1.1.1. installing on Debian

This screenshot shows that there is no **apache** server installed, nor does the **/var/www** directory exist.

```
root@debian7:~# ls -l /var/www
ls: cannot access /var/www: No such file or directory
root@debian7:~# dpkg -l | grep apache
```

To install **apache** on Debian:

```
root@debian7:~# aptitude install apache2
The following NEW packages will be installed:
  apache2 apache2-mpm-worker{a} apache2-utils{a} apache2.2-bin{a} apache2.2-com\
mon{a} libapr1{a} libaprutil1{a} libaprutil1-dbd-sqlite3{a} libaprutil1-ldap{a}\
 ssl-cert{a}
0 packages upgraded, 10 newly installed, 0 to remove and 0 not upgraded.
Need to get 1,487 kB of archives. After unpacking 5,673 kB will be used.
Do you want to continue? [Y/n/?]
```

After installation, the same two commands as above will yield a different result:

```
root@debian7:~# ls -l /var/www
total 4
-rw-r--r-- 1 root root 177 Apr 29 11:55 index.html
root@debian7:~# dpkg -l | grep apache | tr -s ' '
ii apache2 2.2.22-13+deb7u1 amd64 Apache HTTP Server metapackage
ii apache2-mpm-worker 2.2.22-13+deb7u1 amd64 Apache HTTP Server - high speed th\
readed model
ii apache2-utils 2.2.22-13+deb7u1 amd64 utility programs for webservers
ii apache2.2-bin 2.2.22-13+deb7u1 amd64 Apache HTTP Server common binary files
ii apache2.2-common 2.2.22-13+deb7u1 amd64 Apache HTTP Server common files
```

1.1.2. installing on RHEL/CentOS

Note that Red Hat derived distributions use **httpd** as package and process name instead of **apache**.

To verify whether **apache** is installed in CentOS/RHEL:

```
[root@centos65 ~]# rpm -q httpd
package httpd is not installed
[root@centos65 ~]# ls -l /var/www
ls: cannot access /var/www: No such file or directory
```

To install apache on CentOS:

```
[root@centos65 ~]# yum install httpd
```

After running the **yum install httpd** command, the Centos 6.5 server has apache installed and the **/var/www** directory exists.

```
[root@centos65 ~]# rpm -q httpd
httpd-2.2.15-30.el6.centos.x86_64
[root@centos65 ~]# ls -l /var/www
total 16
drwxr-xr-x. 2 root root 4096 Apr  3 23:57 cgi-bin
drwxr-xr-x. 3 root root 4096 May  6 13:08 error
drwxr-xr-x. 2 root root 4096 Apr  3 23:57 html
drwxr-xr-x. 3 root root 4096 May  6 13:08 icons
[root@centos65 ~]#
```

1.1.3. running apache on Debian

This is how you start **apache2** on Debian.

```
root@debian7:~# service apache2 status
Apache2 is NOT running.
root@debian7:~# service apache2 start
Starting web server: apache2apache2: Could not reliably determine the server's \
fully qualified domain name, using 127.0.1.1 for ServerName
.
```

To verify, run the **service apache2 status** command again or use **ps**.

```
root@debian7:~# service apache2 status
Apache2 is running (pid 3680).
root@debian7:~# ps -C apache2
  PID TTY          TIME CMD
 3680 ?        00:00:00 apache2
 3683 ?        00:00:00 apache2
 3684 ?        00:00:00 apache2
 3685 ?        00:00:00 apache2
root@debian7:~#
```

Or use **wget** and **file** to verify that your web server serves an html document.

```
root@debian7:~# wget 127.0.0.1
--2014-05-06 13:27:02--  http://127.0.0.1/
Connecting to 127.0.0.1:80... connected.
HTTP request sent, awaiting response... 200 OK
Length: 177 [text/html]
Saving to: `index.html'

100%[=================================================>] 177     --.-K/s   in 0s

2014-05-06 13:27:02 (15.8 MB/s) - `index.html' saved [177/177]

root@debian7:~# file index.html
index.html: HTML document, ASCII text
root@debian7:~#
```

Or verify that apache is running by opening a web browser, and browse to the ip-address of your server. An Apache test page should be shown.

You can do the following to quickly avoid the 'could not reliably determine the fqdn' message when restarting apache.

```
root@debian7:~# echo ServerName Debian7 >> /etc/apache2/apache2.conf
root@debian7:~# service apache2 restart
Restarting web server: apache2 ... waiting .
root@debian7:~#
```

1.1.4. running apache on CentOS

Starting the **httpd** on RHEL/CentOS is done with the **service** command.

```
[root@centos65 ~]# service httpd status
httpd is stopped
[root@centos65 ~]# service httpd start
Starting httpd: httpd: Could not reliably determine the server's fully qualifie\
d domain name, using 127.0.0.1 for ServerName
                                                          [  OK  ]
[root@centos65 ~]#
```

To verify that **apache** is running, use **ps** or issue the **service httpd status** command again.

```
[root@centos65 ~]# service httpd status
httpd (pid  2410) is running...
[root@centos65 ~]# ps -C httpd
  PID TTY          TIME CMD
 2410 ?        00:00:00 httpd
 2412 ?        00:00:00 httpd
 2413 ?        00:00:00 httpd
 2414 ?        00:00:00 httpd
 2415 ?        00:00:00 httpd
 2416 ?        00.00.00 httpd
 2417 ?        00:00:00 httpd
 2418 ?        00:00:00 httpd
 2419 ?        00:00:00 httpd
[root@centos65 ~]#
```

To prevent the 'Could not reliably determine the fqdn' message, issue the following command.

```
[root@centos65 ~]# echo ServerName Centos65 >> /etc/httpd/conf/httpd.conf
[root@centos65 ~]# service httpd restart
Stopping httpd:                                           [  OK  ]
Starting httpd:                                           [  OK  ]
[root@centos65 ~]#
```

1.1.5. index file on CentOS

CentOS does not provide a standard index.html or index.php file. A simple **wget** gives an error.

```
[root@centos65 ~]# wget 127.0.0.1
--2014-05-06 15:10:22--  http://127.0.0.1/
Connecting to 127.0.0.1:80... connected.
HTTP request sent, awaiting response... 403 Forbidden
2014-05-06 15:10:22 ERROR 403: Forbidden.
```

Instead when visiting the ip-address of your server in a web browser you get a **noindex.html** page. You can verify this using **wget**.

```
[root@centos65 ~]# wget http://127.0.0.1/error/noindex.html
--2014-05-06 15:16:05--  http://127.0.0.1/error/noindex.html
Connecting to 127.0.0.1:80... connected.
HTTP request sent, awaiting response... 200 OK
Length: 5039 (4.9K) [text/html]
Saving to: "noindex.html"

100%[====================================================>] 5,039        --.-K/s   in 0s

2014-05-06 15:16:05 (289 MB/s) - "noindex.html" saved [5039/5039]

[root@centos65 ~]# file noindex.html
noindex.html: HTML document text
[root@centos65 ~]#
```

Any custom **index.html** file in **/var/www/html** will immediately serve as an index for this web server.

```
[root@centos65 ~]# echo 'Welcome to my website' > /var/www/html/index.html
[root@centos65 ~]# wget http://127.0.0.1
--2014-05-06 15:19:16--  http://127.0.0.1/
Connecting to 127.0.0.1:80... connected.
HTTP request sent, awaiting response... 200 OK
Length: 22 [text/html]
Saving to: "index.html"

100%[====================================================>] 22           --.-K/s   in 0s

2014-05-06 15:19:16 (1.95 MB/s) - "index.html" saved [22/22]

[root@centos65 ~]# cat index.html
Welcome to my website
```

1.1.6. default website

Changing the default website of a freshly installed apache web server is easy. All you need to do is create (or change) an index.html file in the DocumentRoot directory.

To locate the DocumentRoot directory on Debian:

```
root@debian7:~# grep DocumentRoot /etc/apache2/sites-available/default
        DocumentRoot /var/www
```

This means that **/var/www/index.html** is the default web site.

```
root@debian7:~# cat /var/www/index.html
<html><body><h1>It works!</h1>
<p>This is the default web page for this server.</p>
<p>The web server software is running but no content has been added, yet.</p>
</body></html>
root@debian7:~#
```

This screenshot shows how to locate the **DocumentRoot** directory on RHEL/CentOS.

```
[root@centos65 ~]# grep ^DocumentRoot /etc/httpd/conf/httpd.conf
DocumentRoot "/var/www/html"
```

RHEL/CentOS have no default web page (only the noindex.html error page mentioned before). But an **index.html** file created in **/var/www/html/** will automatically be used as default page.

```
[root@centos65 ~]# echo '<html><head><title>Default website</title></head><body\
><p>A new web page</p></body></html>' > /var/www/html/index.html
[root@centos65 ~]# cat /var/www/html/index.html
<html><head><title>Default website</title></head><body><p>A new web page</p></b\
ody></html>
[root@centos65 ~]#
```

1.1.7. apache configuration

There are many similarities, but also a couple of differences when configuring **apache** on Debian or on CentOS. Both Linux families will get their own chapters with examples.

All configuration on RHEL/CentOS is done in **/etc/httpd**.

```
[root@centos65 ~]# ls -l /etc/httpd/
total 8
drwxr-xr-x. 2 root root 4096 May  6 13:08 conf
drwxr-xr-x. 2 root root 4096 May  6 13:08 conf.d
lrwxrwxrwx. 1 root root   19 May  6 13:08 logs -> ../../var/log/httpd
lrwxrwxrwx. 1 root root   29 May  6 13:08 modules -> ../../usr/lib64/httpd/modu\
les
lrwxrwxrwx. 1 root root   19 May  6 13:08 run -> ../../var/run/httpd
[root@centos65 ~]#
```

Debian (and ubuntu/mint/...) use **/etc/apache2**.

```
root@debian7:~# ls -l /etc/apache2/
total 72
-rw-r--r-- 1 root root  9659 May  6 14:23 apache2.conf
drwxr-xr-x 2 root root  4096 May  6 13:19 conf.d
-rw-r--r-- 1 root root  1465 Jan 31 18:35 envvars
-rw-r--r-- 1 root root 31063 Jul 20  2013 magic
drwxr-xr-x 2 root root  4096 May  6 13:19 mods-available
drwxr-xr-x 2 root root  4096 May  6 13:19 mods-enabled
-rw-r--r-- 1 root root   750 Jan 26 12:13 ports.conf
drwxr-xr-x 2 root root  4096 May  6 13:19 sites-available
drwxr-xr-x 2 root root  4096 May  6 13:19 sites-enabled
root@debian7:~#
```

1.2. port virtual hosts on Debian

1.2.1. default virtual host

Debian has a virtualhost configuration file for its default website in **/etc/apache2/sites-available/default**.

```
root@debian7:~# head -2 /etc/apache2/sites-available/default
<VirtualHost *:80>
        ServerAdmin webmaster@localhost
```

1.2.2. three extra virtual hosts

In this scenario we create three additional websites for three customers that share a clubhouse and want to jointly hire you. They are a model train club named **Choo Choo**, a chess club named **Chess Club 42** and a hackerspace named **hunter2**.

One way to put three websites on one web server, is to put each website on a different port. This screenshot shows three newly created **virtual hosts**, one for each customer.

```
root@debian7:~# vi /etc/apache2/sites-available/choochoo
root@debian7:~# cat /etc/apache2/sites-available/choochoo
<VirtualHost *:7000>
        ServerAdmin webmaster@localhost
        DocumentRoot /var/www/choochoo
</VirtualHost>
root@debian7:~# vi /etc/apache2/sites-available/chessclub42
root@debian7:~# cat /etc/apache2/sites-available/chessclub42
<VirtualHost *:8000>
        ServerAdmin webmaster@localhost
        DocumentRoot /var/www/chessclub42
</VirtualHost>
root@debian7:~# vi /etc/apache2/sites-available/hunter2
root@debian7:~# cat /etc/apache2/sites-available/hunter2
<VirtualHost *:9000>
        ServerAdmin webmaster@localhost
        DocumentRoot /var/www/hunter2
</VirtualHost>
```

Notice the different port numbers 7000, 8000 and 9000. Notice also that we specified a unique **DocumentRoot** for each website.

Are you using **Ubuntu** or **Mint**, then these configfiles need to end in **.conf**.

1.2.3. three extra ports

We need to enable these three ports on apache in the **ports.conf** file. Open this file with **vi** and add three lines to **listen** on three extra ports.

```
root@debian7:~# vi /etc/apache2/ports.conf
```

Verify with **grep** that the **Listen** directives are added correctly.

```
root@debian7:~# grep ^Listen /etc/apache2/ports.conf
Listen 80
Listen 7000
Listen 8000
Listen 9000
```

1.2.4. three extra websites

Next we need to create three **DocumentRoot** directories.

```
root@debian7:~# mkdir /var/www/choochoo
root@debian7:~# mkdir /var/www/chessclub42
root@debian7:~# mkdir /var/www/hunter2
```

And we have to put some really simple website in those directories.

```
root@debian7:~# echo 'Choo Choo model train Choo Choo' > /var/www/choochoo/inde\
x.html
root@debian7:~# echo 'Welcome to chess club 42' > /var/www/chessclub42/index.ht\
ml
root@debian7:~# echo 'HaCkInG iS fUn At HuNtEr2' > /var/www/hunter2/index.html
```

1.2.5. enabling extra websites

The last step is to enable the websites with the **a2ensite** command. This command will create links in **sites-enabled**.

The links are not there yet...

```
root@debian7:~# cd /etc/apache2/
root@debian7:/etc/apache2# ls sites-available/
chessclub42  choochoo  default  default-ssl  hunter2
root@debian7:/etc/apache2# ls sites-enabled/
000-default
```

So we run the **a2ensite** command for all websites.

```
root@debian7:/etc/apache2# a2ensite choochoo
Enabling site choochoo.
To activate the new configuration, you need to run:
  service apache2 reload
root@debian7:/etc/apache2# a2ensite chessclub42
Enabling site chessclub42.
To activate the new configuration, you need to run:
  service apache2 reload
root@debian7:/etc/apache2# a2ensite hunter2
Enabling site hunter2.
To activate the new configuration, you need to run:
  service apache2 reload
```

The links are created, so we can tell **apache**.

```
root@debian7:/etc/apache2# ls sites-enabled/
000-default  chessclub42  choochoo  hunter2
root@debian7:/etc/apache2# service apache2 reload
Reloading web server config: apache2.
root@debian7:/etc/apache2#
```

1.2.6. testing the three websites

Testing the model train club named **Choo Choo** on port 7000.

```
root@debian7:/etc/apache2# wget 127.0.0.1:7000
--2014-05-06 21:16:03--  http://127.0.0.1:7000/
Connecting to 127.0.0.1:7000... connected.
HTTP request sent, awaiting response... 200 OK
Length: 32 [text/html]
Saving to: `index.html'

100%[===========================================>] 32          --.-K/s   in 0s

2014-05-06 21:16:03 (2.92 MB/s) - `index.html' saved [32/32]

root@debian7:/etc/apache2# cat index.html
Choo Choo model train Choo Choo
```

Testing the chess club named **Chess Club 42** on port 8000.

```
root@debian7:/etc/apache2# wget 127.0.0.1:8000
--2014-05-06 21:16:20--  http://127.0.0.1:8000/
Connecting to 127.0.0.1:8000... connected.
HTTP request sent, awaiting response... 200 OK
Length: 25 [text/html]
Saving to: `index.html.1'

100%[===========================================>] 25          --.-K/s   in 0s

2014-05-06 21:16:20 (2.16 MB/s) - `index.html.1' saved [25/25]

root@debian7:/etc/apache2# cat index.html.1
Welcome to chess club 42
```

Testing the hacker club named **hunter2** on port 9000.

```
root@debian7:/etc/apache2# wget 127.0.0.1:9000
--2014-05-06 21:16:30--  http://127.0.0.1:9000/
Connecting to 127.0.0.1:9000... connected.
HTTP request sent, awaiting response... 200 OK
Length: 26 [text/html]
Saving to: `index.html.2'

100%[===========================================>] 26          --.-K/s   in 0s

2014-05-06 21:16:30 (2.01 MB/s) - `index.html.2' saved [26/26]

root@debian7:/etc/apache2# cat index.html.2
HaCkInG iS fUn At HuNtEr2
```

Cleaning up the temporary files.

```
root@debian7:/etc/apache2# rm index.html index.html.1 index.html.2
```

Try testing from another computer using the ip-address of your server.

1.3. named virtual hosts on Debian

1.3.1. named virtual hosts

The chess club and the model train club find the port numbers too hard to remember. They would prefere to have their website accessible by name.

We continue work on the same server that has three websites on three ports. We need to make sure those websites are accesible using the names **choochoo.local**, **chessclub42.local** and **hunter2.local**.

We start by creating three new virtualhosts.

```
root@debian7:/etc/apache2/sites-available# vi choochoo.local
root@debian7:/etc/apache2/sites-available# vi chessclub42.local
root@debian7:/etc/apache2/sites-available# vi hunter2.local
root@debian7:/etc/apache2/sites-available# cat choochoo.local
<VirtualHost *:80>
        ServerAdmin webmaster@localhost
        ServerName choochoo.local
        DocumentRoot /var/www/choochoo
</VirtualHost>
root@debian7:/etc/apache2/sites-available# cat chessclub42.local
<VirtualHost *:80>
        ServerAdmin webmaster@localhost
        ServerName chessclub42.local
        DocumentRoot /var/www/chessclub42
</VirtualHost>
root@debian7:/etc/apache2/sites-available# cat hunter2.local
<VirtualHost *:80>
        ServerAdmin webmaster@localhost
        ServerName hunter2.local
        DocumentRoot /var/www/hunter2
</VirtualHost>
root@debian7:/etc/apache2/sites-available#
```

Notice that they all listen on **port 80** and have an extra **ServerName** directive.

1.3.2. name resolution

We need some way to resolve names. This can be done with DNS, which is discussed in another chapter. For this demo it is also possible to quickly add the three names to the **/etc/hosts** file.

```
root@debian7:/etc/apache2/sites-available# grep ^192 /etc/hosts
192.168.42.50 choochoo.local
192.168.42.50 chessclub42.local
192.168.42.50 hunter2.local
```

Note that you may have another ip address...

1.3.3. enabling virtual hosts

Next we enable them with **a2ensite**.

```
root@debian7:/etc/apache2/sites-available# a2ensite choochoo.local
Enabling site choochoo.local.
To activate the new configuration, you need to run:
  service apache2 reload
root@debian7:/etc/apache2/sites-available# a2ensite chessclub42.local
Enabling site chessclub42.local.
To activate the new configuration, you need to run:
  service apache2 reload
root@debian7:/etc/apache2/sites-available# a2ensite hunter2.local
Enabling site hunter2.local.
To activate the new configuration, you need to run:
  service apache2 reload
```

1.3.4. reload and verify

After a **service apache2 reload** the websites should be available by name.

```
root@debian7:/etc/apache2/sites-available# service apache2 reload
Reloading web server config: apache2.
root@debian7:/etc/apache2/sites-available# wget chessclub42.local
--2014-05-06 21:37:13--  http://chessclub42.local/
Resolving chessclub42.local (chessclub42.local)... 192.168.42.50
Connecting to chessclub42.local (chessclub42.local)|192.168.42.50|:80... conne\
cted.
HTTP request sent, awaiting response... 200 OK
Length: 25 [text/html]
Saving to: `index.html'

100%[=============================================>] 25          --.-K/s    in 0s

2014-05-06 21:37:13 (2.06 MB/s) - `index.html' saved [25/25]

root@debian7:/etc/apache2/sites-available# cat index.html
Welcome to chess club 42
```

1.4. password protected website on Debian

You can secure files and directories in your website with a **.htaccess** file that refers to a **.htpasswd** file. The **htpasswd** command can create a **.htpasswd** file that contains a userid and an (encrypted) password.

This screenshot creates a user and password for the hacker named **cliff** and uses the **-c** flag to create the **.htpasswd** file.

```
root@debian7:~# htpasswd -c /var/www/.htpasswd cliff
New password:
Re-type new password:
Adding password for user cliff
root@debian7:~# cat /var/www/.htpasswd
cliff:$apr1$vujll0KL$./SZ4w9q0swhX93pQ0PVp.
```

Hacker **rob** also wants access, this screenshot shows how to add a second user and password to **.htpasswd**.

```
root@debian7:~# htpasswd /var/www/.htpasswd rob
New password:
Re-type new password:
Adding password for user rob
root@debian7:~# cat /var/www/.htpasswd
cliff:$apr1$vujll0KL$./SZ4w9q0swhX93pQ0PVp.
rob:$apr1$HNln1FFt$nR1pF0H.IW11/1DRq41Qo0
```

Both Cliff and Rob chose the same password (hunter2), but that is not visible in the **.htpasswd** file because of the different salts.

Next we need to create a **.htaccess** file in the **DocumentRoot** of the website we want to protect. This screenshot shows an example.

```
root@debian7:~# cd /var/www/hunter2/
root@debian7:/var/www/hunter2# cat .htaccess
AuthUserFile /var/www/.htpasswd
AuthName "Members only!"
AuthType Basic
require valid-user
```

Note that we are protecting the website on **port 9000** that we created earlier.

And because we put the website for the Hackerspace named hunter2 in a subdirectory of the default website, we will need to adjust the **AllowOvveride** parameter in **/etc/apache2/sites-available/default** as this screenshot shows (with line numbers on Debian7, your may vary).

```
9          <Directory /var/www/>
10              Options Indexes FollowSymLinks MultiViews
11              AllowOverride Authconfig
12              Order allow,deny
13              allow from all
14         </Directory>
```

Now restart the apache2 server and test that it works!

1.5. port virtual hosts on CentOS

1.5.1. default virtual host

Unlike Debian, CentOS has no virtualHost configuration file for its default website. Instead the default configuration will throw a standard error page when no index file can be found in the default location (/var/www/html).

1.5.2. three extra virtual hosts

In this scenario we create three additional websites for three customers that share a clubhouse and want to jointly hire you. They are a model train club named **Choo Choo**, a chess club named **Chess Club 42** and a hackerspace named **hunter2**.

One way to put three websites on one web server, is to put each website on a different port. This screenshot shows three newly created **virtual hosts**, one for each customer.

```
[root@CentOS65 ~]# vi /etc/httpd/conf.d/choochoo.conf
[root@CentOS65 ~]# cat /etc/httpd/conf.d/choochoo.conf
<VirtualHost *:7000>
        ServerAdmin webmaster@localhost
        DocumentRoot /var/www/html/choochoo
</VirtualHost>
[root@CentOS65 ~]# vi /etc/httpd/conf.d/chessclub42.conf
[root@CentOS65 ~]# cat /etc/httpd/conf.d/chessclub42.conf
<VirtualHost *:8000>
        ServerAdmin webmaster@localhost
        DocumentRoot /var/www/html/chessclub42
</VirtualHost>
[root@CentOS65 ~]# vi /etc/httpd/conf.d/hunter2.conf
[root@CentOS65 ~]# cat /etc/httpd/conf.d/hunter2.conf
<VirtualHost *:9000>
        ServerAdmin webmaster@localhost
        DocumentRoot /var/www/html/hunter2
</VirtualHost>
```

Notice the different port numbers 7000, 8000 and 9000. Notice also that we specified a unique **DocumentRoot** for each website.

1.5.3. three extra ports

We need to enable these three ports on apache in the **httpd.conf** file.

```
[root@CentOS65 ~]# vi /etc/httpd/conf/httpd.conf
root@debian7:~# grep ^Listen /etc/httpd/conf/httpd.conf
Listen 80
Listen 7000
Listen 8000
Listen 9000
```

1.5.4. SELinux guards our ports

If we try to restart our server, we will notice the following error:

```
[root@CentOS65 ~]# service httpd restart
Stopping httpd:                                          [  OK  ]
Starting httpd:
       (13)Permission denied: make_sock: could not bind to address 0.0.0.0:7000
no listening sockets available, shutting down
                                                         [FAILED]
```

This is due to SELinux reserving ports 7000 and 8000 for other uses. We need to tell SELinux we want to use these ports for http traffic

```
[root@CentOS65 ~]# semanage port -m -t http_port_t -p tcp 7000
[root@CentOS65 ~]# semanage port -m -t http_port_t -p tcp 8000
[root@CentOS65 ~]# service httpd restart
Stopping httpd:                                          [  OK  ]
Starting httpd:                                          [  OK  ]
```

1.5.5. three extra websites

Next we need to create three **DocumentRoot** directories.

```
[root@CentOS65 ~]# mkdir /var/www/html/choochoo
[root@CentOS65 ~]# mkdir /var/www/html/chessclub42
[root@CentOS65 ~]# mkdir /var/www/html/hunter2
```

And we have to put some really simple website in those directories.

```
[root@CentOS65 ~]# echo 'Choo Choo model train Choo Choo' > /var/www/html/chooc\
hoo/index.html
[root@CentOS65 ~]# echo 'Welcome to chess club 42' > /var/www/html/chessclub42/\
index.html
[root@CentOS65 ~]# echo 'HaCkInG iS fUn At HuNtEr2' > /var/www/html/hunter2/ind\
ex.html
```

1.5.6. enabling extra websites

The only way to enable or disable configurations in RHEL/CentOS is by renaming or moving the configuration files. Any file in /etc/httpd/conf.d ending on .conf will be loaded by Apache. To disable a site we can either rename the file or move it to another directory.

The files are created, so we can tell **apache**.

```
[root@CentOS65 ~]# ls /etc/httpd/conf.d/
chessclub42.conf  choochoo.conf  hunter2.conf  README  welcome.conf
[root@CentOS65 ~]# service httpd reload
Reloading httpd:
```

1.5.7. testing the three websites

Testing the model train club named **Choo Choo** on port 7000.

```
[root@CentOS65 ~]# wget 127.0.0.1:7000
--2014-05-11 11:59:36--  http://127.0.0.1:7000/
Connecting to 127.0.0.1:7000... connected.
HTTP request sent, awaiting response... 200 OK
Length: 32 [text/html]
Saving to: `index.html'

100%[==============================================>] 32          --.-K/s   in 0s

2014-05-11 11:59:36 (4.47 MB/s) - `index.html' saved [32/32]

[root@CentOS65 ~]# cat index.html
Choo Choo model train Choo Choo
```

Testing the chess club named **Chess Club 42** on port 8000.

```
[root@CentOS65 ~]# wget 127.0.0.1:8000
--2014-05-11 12:01:30--  http://127.0.0.1:8000/
Connecting to 127.0.0.1:8000... connected.
HTTP request sent, awaiting response... 200 OK
Length: 25 [text/html]
Saving to: `index.html.1'

100%[==============================================>] 25          --.-K/s   in 0s

2014-05-11 12:01:30 (4.25 MB/s) - `index.html.1' saved [25/25]

root@debian7:/etc/apache2# cat index.html.1
Welcome to chess club 42
```

Testing the hacker club named **hunter2** on port 9000.

```
[root@CentOS65 ~]# wget 127.0.0.1:9000
--2014-05-11 12:02:37--  http://127.0.0.1:9000/
Connecting to 127.0.0.1:9000... connected.
HTTP request sent, awaiting response... 200 OK
Length: 26 [text/html]
Saving to: `index.html.2'

100%[==============================================>] 26          --.-K/s   in 0s

2014-05-11 12:02:37 (4.49 MB/s) - `index.html.2' saved [26/26]

root@debian7:/etc/apache2# cat index.html.2
HaCkInG iS fUn At HuNtEr2
```

Cleaning up the temporary files.

```
[root@CentOS65 ~]# rm index.html index.html.1 index.html.2
```

1.5.8. firewall rules

If we attempt to access the site from another machine however, we will not be able to view the website yet. The firewall is blocking incoming connections. We need to open these incoming ports first

```
[root@CentOS65 ~]# iptables -I INPUT -p tcp --dport 80 -j ACCEPT
[root@CentOS65 ~]# iptables -I INPUT -p tcp --dport 7000 -j ACCEPT
[root@CentOS65 ~]# iptables -I INPUT -p tcp --dport 8000 -j ACCEPT
[root@CentOS65 ~]# iptables -I INPUT -p tcp --dport 9000 -j ACCEPT
```

And if we want these rules to remain active after a reboot, we need to save them

```
[root@CentOS65 ~]# service iptables save
iptables: Saving firewall rules to /etc/sysconfig/iptables:[  OK  ]
```

1.6. named virtual hosts on CentOS

1.6.1. named virtual hosts

The chess club and the model train club find the port numbers too hard to remember. They would prefere to have their website accessible by name.

We continue work on the same server that has three websites on three ports. We need to make sure those websites are accesible using the names **choochoo.local**, **chessclub42.local** and **hunter2.local**.

First, we need to enable named virtual hosts in the configuration

```
[root@CentOS65 ~]# vi /etc/httpd/conf/httpd.conf
[root@CentOS65 ~]# grep ^NameVirtualHost /etc/httpd/conf/httpd.conf
NameVirtualHost *:80
[root@CentOS65 ~]#
```

Next we need to create three new virtualhosts.

```
[root@CentOS65 ~]# vi /etc/httpd/conf.d/choochoo.local.conf
[root@CentOS65 ~]# vi /etc/httpd/conf.d/chessclub42.local.conf
[root@CentOS65 ~]# vi /etc/httpd/conf.d/hunter2.local.conf
[root@CentOS65 ~]# cat /etc/httpd/conf.d/choochoo.local.conf
<VirtualHost *:80>
        ServerAdmin webmaster@localhost
        ServerName choochoo.local
        DocumentRoot /var/www/html/choochoo
</VirtualHost>
[root@CentOS65 ~]# cat /etc/httpd/conf.d/chessclub42.local.conf
<VirtualHost *:80>
        ServerAdmin webmaster@localhost
        ServerName chessclub42.local
        DocumentRoot /var/www/html/chessclub42
</VirtualHost>
[root@CentOS65 ~]# cat /etc/httpd/conf.d/hunter2.local.conf
<VirtualHost *:80>
        ServerAdmin webmaster@localhost
        ServerName hunter2.local
        DocumentRoot /var/www/html/hunter2
</VirtualHost>
[root@CentOS65 ~]#
```

Notice that they all listen on **port 80** and have an extra **ServerName** directive.

1.6.2. name resolution

We need some way to resolve names. This can be done with DNS, which is discussed in another chapter. For this demo it is also possible to quickly add the three names to the **/etc/hosts** file.

```
[root@CentOS65 ~]# grep ^192 /etc/hosts
192.168.1.225 choochoo.local
192.168.1.225 chessclub42.local
192.168.1.225 hunter2.local
```

Note that you may have another ip address...

1.6.3. reload and verify

After a **service httpd reload** the websites should be available by name.

```
[root@CentOS65 ~]# service httpd reload
Reloading httpd:
[root@CentOS65 ~]# wget chessclub42.local
--2014-05-25 16:59:14--  http://chessclub42.local/
Resolving chessclub42.local... 192.168.1.225
Connecting to chessclub42.local|192.168.1.225|:80... connected.
HTTP request sent, awaiting response... 200 OK
Length: 25 [text/html]
Saving to: âindex.htmlâ

100%[=============================================>] 25          --.-K/s   in 0s

2014-05-25 16:59:15 (1014 KB/s) - `index.html' saved [25/25]

[root@CentOS65 ~]# cat index.html
Welcome to chess club 42
```

1.7. password protected website on CentOS

You can secure files and directories in your website with a **.htaccess** file that refers to a **.htpasswd** file. The **htpasswd** command can create a **.htpasswd** file that contains a userid and an (encrypted) password.

This screenshot creates a user and password for the hacker named **cliff** and uses the **-c** flag to create the **.htpasswd** file.

```
[root@CentOS65 ~]# htpasswd -c /var/www/.htpasswd cliff
New password:
Re-type new password:
Adding password for user cliff
[root@CentOS65 ~]# cat /var/www/.htpasswd
cliff:QNwTrymMLBctU
```

Hacker **rob** also wants access, this screenshot shows how to add a second user and password to **.htpasswd**.

```
[root@CentOS65 ~]# htpasswd /var/www/.htpasswd rob
New password:
Re-type new password:
Adding password for user rob
[root@CentOS65 ~]# cat /var/www/.htpasswd
cliff:QNwTrymMLBctU
rob:EC2vOCcrMXDoM
[root@CentOS65 ~]#
```

Both Cliff and Rob chose the same password (hunter2), but that is not visible in the **.htpasswd** file because of the different salts.

Next we need to create a **.htaccess** file in the **DocumentRoot** of the website we want to protect. This screenshot shows an example.

```
[root@CentOS65 ~]# cat /var/www/html/hunter2/.htaccess
AuthUserFile /var/www/.htpasswd
AuthName "Members only!"
AuthType Basic
require valid-user
```

Note that we are protecting the website on **port 9000** that we created earlier.

And because we put the website for the Hackerspace named hunter2 in a subdirectory of the default website, we will need to adjust the **AllowOvveride** parameter in **/etc/httpd/conf/httpd.conf** under the **<Directory "/var/www/html">** directive as this screenshot shows.

```
[root@CentOS65 ~]# vi /etc/httpd/conf/httpd.conf

<Directory "/var/www/html">

#
# Possible values for the Options directive are "None", "All",
# or any combination of:
#   Indexes Includes FollowSymLinks SymLinksifOwnerMatch ExecCGI MultiViews
#
# Note that "MultiViews" must be named *explicitly* --- "Options All"
# doesn't give it to you.
#
# The Options directive is both complicated and important.  Please see
# http://httpd.apache.org/docs/2.2/mod/core.html#options
# for more information.
#
    Options Indexes FollowSymLinks


#
# AllowOverride controls what directives may be placed in .htaccess files.
# It can be "All", "None", or any combination of the keywords:
#   Options FileInfo AuthConfig Limit
#
    AllowOverride Authconfig


#
# Controls who can get stuff from this server.
#
    Order allow,deny
    Allow from all

</Directory>
```

Now restart the apache2 server and test that it works!

1.8. troubleshooting apache

When apache restarts, it will verify the syntax of files in the configuration folder **/etc/apache2** on debian or **/etc/httpd** on CentOS and it will tell you the name of the faulty file, the line number and an explanation of the error.

```
root@debian7:~# service apache2 restart
apache2: Syntax error on line 268 of /etc/apache2/apache2.conf: Syntax error o\
n line 1 of /etc/apache2/sites-enabled/chessclub42: /etc/apache2/sites-enabled\
/chessclub42:4: <VirtualHost> was not closed.\n/etc/apache2/sites-enabled/ches\
sclub42:1: <VirtualHost> was not closed.
Action 'configtest' failed.
The Apache error log may have more information.
 failed!
```

Below you see the problem... a missing / before on line 4.

```
root@debian7:~# cat /etc/apache2/sites-available/chessclub42
<VirtualHost *:8000>
        ServerAdmin webmaster@localhost
        DocumentRoot /var/www/chessclub42
<VirtualHost>
```

Let us force another error by renaming the directory of one of our websites:

```
root@debian7:~# mv /var/www/choochoo/ /var/www/chooshoo
root@debian7:~# !ser
service apache2 restart
Restarting web server: apache2Warning: DocumentRoot [/var/www/choochoo] does n\
ot exist
Warning: DocumentRoot [/var/www/choochoo] does not exist
 ... waiting Warning: DocumentRoot [/var/www/choochoo] does not exist
Warning: DocumentRoot [/var/www/choochoo] does not exist
 .
```

As you can see, apache will tell you exactly what is wrong.

You can also troubleshoot by connecting to the website via a browser and then checking the apache log files in **/var/log/apache**.

1.9. virtual hosts example

Below is a sample virtual host configuration. This virtual hosts overrules the default Apache **ErrorDocument** directive.

```
<VirtualHost 83.217.76.245:80>
ServerName cobbaut.be
ServerAlias www.cobbaut.be
DocumentRoot /home/paul/public_html
ErrorLog /home/paul/logs/error_log
CustomLog /home/paul/logs/access_log common
ScriptAlias /cgi-bin/ /home/paul/cgi-bin/
<Directory /home/paul/public_html>
 Options Indexes IncludesNOEXEC FollowSymLinks
 allow from all
</Directory>
ErrorDocument 404 http://www.cobbaut.be/cobbaut.php
</VirtualHost>
```

1.10. aliases and redirects

Apache supports aliases for directories, like this example shows.

```
Alias /paul/ "/home/paul/public_html/"
```

Similarly, content can be redirected to another website or web server.

```
Redirect permanent /foo http://www.foo.com/bar
```

1.11. more on .htaccess

You can do much more with **.htaccess**. One example is to use .htaccess to prevent people from certain domains to access your website. Like in this case, where a number of referer spammers are blocked from the website.

```
paul@lounge:~/cobbaut.be$ cat .htaccess
# Options +FollowSymlinks
RewriteEngine On
RewriteCond %{HTTP_REFERER} ^http://(www\.)?buy-adipex.fw.nu.*$ [OR]
RewriteCond %{HTTP_REFERER} ^http://(www\.)?buy-levitra.asso.ws.*$ [NC,OR]
RewriteCond %{HTTP_REFERER} ^http://(www\.)?buy-tramadol.fw.nu.*$ [NC,OR]
RewriteCond %{HTTP_REFERER} ^http://(www\.)?buy-viagra.lookin.at.*$ [NC,OR]
...
RewriteCond %{HTTP_REFERER} ^http://(www\.)?www.healthinsurancehelp.net.*$ [NC]
RewriteRule .* - [F,L]
paul@lounge:~/cobbaut.be$
```

1.12. traffic

Apache keeps a log of all visitors. The **webalizer** is often used to parse this log into nice html statistics.

1.13. self signed cert on Debian

Below is a very quick guide on setting up Apache2 on Debian 7 with a self-signed certificate.

Chances are these packages are already installed.

```
root@debian7:~# aptitude install apache2 openssl
No packages will be installed, upgraded, or removed.
0 packages upgraded, 0 newly installed, 0 to remove and 0 not upgraded.
Need to get 0 B of archives. After unpacking 0 B will be used.
```

Create a directory to store the certs, and use **openssl** to create a self signed cert that is valid for 999 days.

```
root@debian7:~# mkdir /etc/ssl/localcerts
root@debian7:~# openssl req -new -x509 -days 999 -nodes -out /etc/ssl/local\
certs/apache.pem -keyout /etc/ssl/localcerts/apache.key
Generating a 2048 bit RSA private key
...
...
writing new private key to '/etc/ssl/localcerts/apache.key'
-----
You are about to be asked to enter information that will be incorporated
into your certificate request.
What you are about to enter is what is called a Distinguished Name or a DN.
There are quite a few fields but you can leave some blank
For some fields there will be a default value,
If you enter '.', the field will be left blank.
-----
Country Name (2 letter code) [AU]:BE
State or Province Name (full name) [Some-State]:Antwerp
Locality Name (eg, city) []:Antwerp
Organization Name (eg, company) [Internet Widgits Pty Ltd]:linux-training.be
Organizational Unit Name (eg, section) []:
Common Name (e.g. server FQDN or YOUR name) []:Paul
Email Address []:
```

A little security never hurt anyone.

```
root@debian7:~# ls -l /etc/ssl/localcerts/
total 8
-rw-r--r-- 1 root root 1704 Sep 16 18:24 apache.key
-rw-r--r-- 1 root root 1302 Sep 16 18:24 apache.pem
root@debian7:~# chmod 600 /etc/ssl/localcerts/*
root@debian7:~# ls -l /etc/ssl/localcerts/
total 8
-rw------- 1 root root 1704 Sep 16 18:24 apache.key
-rw------- 1 root root 1302 Sep 16 18:24 apache.pem
```

Enable the **apache ssl mod**.

```
root@debian7:~# a2enmod ssl
Enabling module ssl.
See /usr/share/doc/apache2.2-common/README.Debian.gz on how to configure SSL\
 and create self-signed certificates.
To activate the new configuration, you need to run:
  service apache2 restart
```

Create the website configuration.

```
root@debian7:~# vi /etc/apache2/sites-available/choochoos
```

```
root@debian7:~# cat /etc/apache2/sites-available/choochoos
<VirtualHost *:7000>
        ServerAdmin webmaster@localhost
        DocumentRoot /var/www/choochoos
        SSLEngine On
        SSLCertificateFile /etc/ssl/localcerts/apache.pem
        SSLCertificateKeyFile /etc/ssl/localcerts/apache.key
</VirtualHost>
root@debian7:~#
```

And create the website itself.

```
root@debian7:/var/www/choochoos# vi index.html
root@debian7:/var/www/choochoos# cat index.html
Choo Choo HTTPS secured model train Choo Choo
```

Enable the website and restart (or reload) apache2.

```
root@debian7:/var/www/choochoos# a2ensite choochoos
Enabling site choochoos.
To activate the new configuration, you need to run:
  service apache2 reload
root@debian7:/var/www/choochoos# service apache2 restart
Restarting web server: apache2 ... waiting .
```

Chances are your browser will warn you about the self signed certificate.

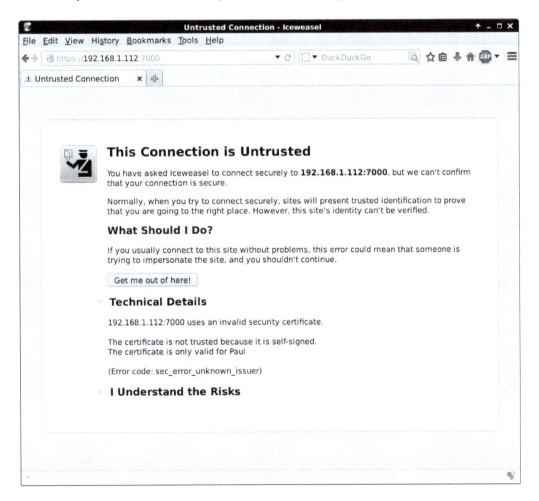

1.14. self signed cert on RHEL/CentOS

Below is a quick way to create a self signed cert for https on RHEL/CentOS. You may need these packages:

```
[root@paulserver ~]# yum install httpd openssl mod_ssl
Loaded plugins: fastestmirror
Loading mirror speeds from cached hostfile
 * base: ftp.belnet.be
 * extras: ftp.belnet.be
 * updates: mirrors.vooservers.com
base                                              | 3.7 kB     00:00
Setting up Install Process
Package httpd-2.2.15-31.el6.centos.x86_64 already installed and latest version
Package openssl-1.0.1e-16.el6_5.15.x86_64 already installed and latest version
Package 1:mod_ssl-2.2.15-31.el6.centos.x86_64 already ins... and latest version
Nothing to do
```

We use **openssl** to create the certificate.

```
[root@paulserver ~]# mkdir certs
[root@paulserver ~]# cd certs
[root@paulserver certs]# openssl genrsa -out ca.key 2048
Generating RSA private key, 2048 bit long modulus
.........+++
.......................................................+++
e is 65537 (0x10001)
[root@paulserver certs]# openssl req -new -key ca.key -out ca.csr
You are about to be asked to enter information that will be incorporated
into your certificate request.
What you are about to enter is what is called a Distinguished Name or a DN.
There are quite a few fields but you can leave some blank
For some fields there will be a default value,
If you enter '.', the field will be left blank.
-----
Country Name (2 letter code) [XX]:BE
State or Province Name (full name) []:antwerp
Locality Name (eg, city) [Default City]:antwerp
Organization Name (eg, company) [Default Company Ltd]:antwerp
Organizational Unit Name (eg, section) []:
Common Name (eg, your name or your server's hostname) []:paulserver
Email Address []:

Please enter the following 'extra' attributes
to be sent with your certificate request
A challenge password []:
An optional company name []:
[root@paulserver certs]# openssl x509 -req -days 365 -in ca.csr -signkey ca.ke\
y -out ca.crt
Signature ok
subject=/C=BE/ST=antwerp/L=antwerp/O=antwerp/CN=paulserver
Getting Private key
```

We copy the keys to the right location (You may be missing SELinux info here).

```
[root@paulserver certs]# cp ca.crt /etc/pki/tls/certs/
[root@paulserver certs]# cp ca.key ca.csr /etc/pki/tls/private/
```

We add the location of our keys to this file, and also add the **NameVirtualHost *:443** directive.

```
[root@paulserver certs]# vi /etc/httpd/conf.d/ssl.conf
```

```
[root@paulserver certs]# grep ^SSLCerti /etc/httpd/conf.d/ssl.conf
SSLCertificateFile /etc/pki/tls/certs/ca.crt
SSLCertificateKeyFile /etc/pki/tls/private/ca.key
```

Create a website configuration.

```
[root@paulserver certs]# vi /etc/httpd/conf.d/choochoos.conf
[root@paulserver certs]# cat /etc/httpd/conf.d/choochoos.conf
<VirtualHost *:443>
        SSLEngine on
        SSLCertificateFile /etc/pki/tls/certs/ca.crt
        SSLCertificateKeyFile /etc/pki/tls/private/ca.key
        DocumentRoot /var/www/choochoos
        ServerName paulserver
</VirtualHost>
[root@paulserver certs]#
```

Create a simple website and restart apache.

```
[root@paulserver certs]# mkdir /var/www/choochoos
[root@paulserver certs]# echo HTTPS model train choochoos > /var/www/choochoos/\
index.html
[root@paulserver httpd]# service httpd restart
Stopping httpd:                                        [  OK  ]
Starting httpd:                                        [  OK  ]
```

And your browser will probably warn you that this certificate is self signed.

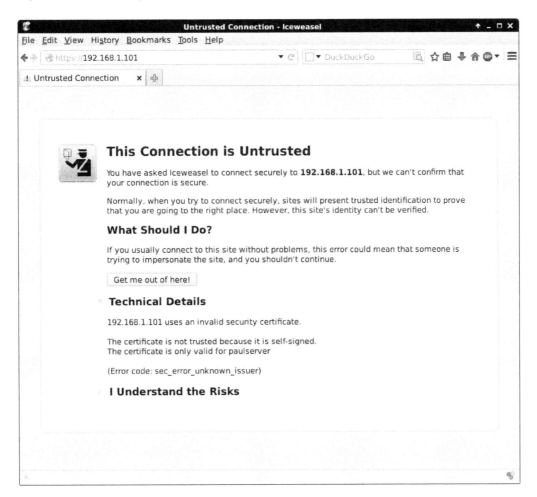

1.15. practice: apache

1. Verify that Apache is installed and running.

2. Browse to the Apache HTML manual.

3. Create three virtual hosts that listen on ports 8472, 31337 and 1201. Test that it all works.

4. Create three named virtual hosts startrek.local, starwars.local and stargate.local. Test that it all works.

5. Create a virtual hosts that listens on another ip-address.

6. Protect one of your websites with a user/password combo.

Chapter 2. introduction to squid

2.1. about proxy servers

2.1.1. usage

A **proxy server** is a server that caches the internet. Clients connect to the proxy server with a request for an internet server. The proxy server will connect to the internet server on behalf of the client. The proxy server will also cache the pages retrieved from the internet server. A proxy server may provide pages from his cache to a client, instead of connecting to the internet server to retrieve the (same) pages.

A proxy server has two main advantages. It improves web surfing speed when returning cached data to clients, and it reduces the required bandwidth (cost) to the internet.

Smaller organizations sometimes put the proxy server on the same physical computer that serves as a NAT to the internet. In larger organizations, the proxy server is one of many servers in the DMZ.

When web traffic passes via a proxy server, it is common practice to configure the proxy with extra settings for access control. Access control in a proxy server can mean user account access, but also website(url), ip-address or dns restrictions.

2.1.2. open proxy servers

You can find lists of open proxy servers on the internet that enable you to surf anonymously. This works when the proxy server connects on your behalf to a website, without logging your ip-address. But be careful, these (listed) open proxy servers could be created in order to eavesdrop upon their users.

2.1.3. squid

This module is an introduction to the **squid** proxy server (http://www.squid-cache.org). We will first configure squid as a normal proxy server.

2.2. installing squid

This screenshot shows how to install squid on Debian with **aptitude**. Use **yum** if you are on Red Hat/CentOS.

```
root@debian7:~# aptitude install squid
The following NEW packages will be installed:
  squid squid-common{a} squid-langpack{a}
0 packages upgraded, 3 newly installed, 0 to remove and 0 not upgraded.
Need to get 1,513 kB of archives. After unpacking 4,540 kB will be used.
Do you want to continue? [Y/n/?]
...output truncated...
Setting up squid-langpack (20120616-1) ...
Setting up squid-common (2.7.STABLE9-4.1) ...
Setting up squid (2.7.STABLE9-4.1) ...
Creating squid spool directory structure
2014/08/01 15:19:31| Creating Swap Directories
Restarting Squid HTTP proxy: squid.
```

squid's main configuration file is **/etc/squid/squid.conf**. The file explains every parameter in great detail.

```
root@debian7:~# wc -l /etc/squid/squid.conf
4948 /etc/squid/squid.conf
```

2.3. port 3128

By default the **squid proxy server** will lsiten to **port 3128**.

```
root@debian7:~# grep ^http_port /etc/squid/squid.conf
http_port 3128
root@debian7:~#
```

2.4. starting and stopping

You can manage **squid** with the standard **service** command as shown in this screenshot.

```
root@debian7:~# service squid start
Starting Squid HTTP proxy: squid.
root@debian7:~# service squid restart
Restarting Squid HTTP proxy: squid.
root@debian7:~# service squid status
squid is running.
root@debian7:~# service squid stop
Stopping Squid HTTP proxy: squid.
root@debian7:~#
```

2.5. client proxy settings

To enable a proxy server in **Firefox** or **Iceweasel** go to **Edit Preferences** and configure as shown in this screenshot (replace 192.168.1.60 with the ip address of your proxy server).

Test that your internet works with the proxy enabled. Also test that after a **service squid stop** command on your proxy server that you get a message similar to this schreenshot.

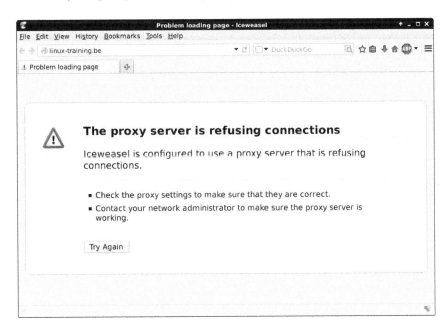

To enable a proxy server with Google Chrome (or Debian Chromium) start the program from the command line like this:

```
paul@debian7:~$ chromium --proxy-server='192.168.1.60:3128'
```

Disabling the proxy with **service squid stop** should result in an error message similar to this screenshot.

2.6. upside down images

A proxy server sits inbetween your browser and the internet. So besides caching of internet data (the original function of a proxy server) and besides firewall like restrictions based on www content, a proxy server is in the perfect position to alter the webpages that you visit.

You could for instance change the advertising on a webpage (or remove certain advertisers), or like we do in this example; change all images so they are upside down.

The server needs command line tools to manipulate images and a perl script that uses these tools (and **wget** to download the images locally and serve them with **apache2**). In this example we use **imagemagick** (which provides tools like **convert** and **mogrify**).

```
root@debian7:~# aptitude install imagemagick wget perl apache2
...output truncated...
root@debian7:~# dpkg -S $(readlink -f $(which mogrify))
imagemagick: /usr/bin/mogrify.im6
root@debian7:~#
```

The perl script that is shown in the screenshot below can be found on several websites, yet I have not found the original author. It is however a very simple script that uses **wget** and **mogrify** to download images (.jpg .gif and .png), flip them and store them in **/var/www/images**.

```
root@debian7:~# cat /usr/local/bin/flip.pl
#!/usr/bin/perl
$|=1;
$count = 0;
$pid = $$;
while (<>) {
 chomp $_;
 if ($_ =~ /(.*\.jpg)/i) {
  $url = $1;
  system("/usr/bin/wget", "-q", "-O","/var/www/images/$pid-$count.jpg", "$url");
  system("/usr/bin/mogrify", "-flip","/var/www/images/$pid-$count.jpg");
  print "http://127.0.0.1/images/$pid-$count.jpg\n";
 }
 elsif ($_ =~ /(.*\.gif)/i) {
  $url = $1;
  system("/usr/bin/wget", "-q", "-O","/var/www/images/$pid-$count.gif", "$url");
  system("/usr/bin/mogrify", "-flip","/var/www/images/$pid-$count.gif");
  print "http://127.0.0.1/images/$pid-$count.gif\n";
 }
 elsif ($_ =~ /(.*\.png)/i) {
  $url = $1;
  system("/usr/bin/wget", "-q", "-O","/var/www/images/$pid-$count.png", "$url");
  system("/usr/bin/mogrify", "-flip","/var/www/images/$pid-$count.png");
  print "http://127.0.0.1/images/$pid-$count.png\n";
 }
 else {
        print "$_\n";;
 }
 $count++;
}
```

Change (or enable) also the following line in **/etc/squid/suiqd.conf**.

```
http_access allow localnet
http_port 3128 transparent
```

```
url_rwwrite_program /usr/local/bin/flip.pl
```

The directory this script uses is **/var/www/images** and should be accessible by both the **squid server** (which uses the user named **proxy** and by the **apache2** webserver (which uses the user **www-data**. The screenshot below shows how to create this directory, set the permissions and make the users a member of the other groups.

```
root@debian7:~# mkdir /var/www/images
root@debian7:~# chown www-data:www-data /var/www/images
root@debian7:~# chmod 755 /var/www/images
root@debian7:~# usermod -aG www-data proxy
root@debian7:~# usermod -aG proxy www-data
```

Test that it works after restarting **squid** and **apache2**.

2.7. /var/log/squid

The standard log file location for squid is **/var/log/squid**.

```
[root@RHEL4 ~]# grep "/var/log" /etc/squid/squid.conf
# cache_access_log /var/log/squid/access.log
# cache_log /var/log/squid/cache.log
# cache_store_log /var/log/squid/store.log
```

2.8. access control

The default squid setup only allows localhost access. To enable access for a private network range, look for the "INSERT YOUR OWN RULE(S) HERE..." sentence in squid.conf and add two lines similar to the screenshot below.

```
# INSERT YOUR OWN RULE(S) HERE TO ALLOW ACCESS FROM YOUR CLIENTS

acl company_network src 192.168.1.0/24
http_access allow company_network
```

2.9. testing squid

First, make sure that the server running squid has access to the internet.

```
[root@RHEL4 ~]# wget -q http://linux-training.be/index.html
[root@RHEL4 ~]# ls -l index.html
-rw-r--r-- 1 root root 2269 Sep 18 13:18 index.html
[root@RHEL4 ~]#
```

Then configure a browser on a client to use the proxy server, or you could set the HTTP_PROXY (sometimes http_proxy) variable to point command line programs to the proxy.

```
[root@fedora ~]# export HTTP_PROXY=http://192.168.1.39:8080
[root@ubuntu ~]# export http_proxy=http://192.168.1.39:8080
```

Testing a client machine can then be done with wget (wget -q is used to simplify the screenshot).

```
[root@RHEL5 ~]# > /etc/resolv.conf
[root@RHEL5 ~]# wget -q http://www.linux-training.be/index.html
[root@RHEL5 ~]# ls -l index.html
-rw-r--r-- 1 root root 2269 Sep 18  2008 index.html
[root@RHEL5 ~]#
```

2.10. name resolution

You need name resolution working on the **squid** server, but you don't need name resolution on the clients.

```
[paul@RHEL5 ~]$ wget http://grep.be
--14:35:44--  http://grep.be
Resolving grep.be... failed: Temporary failure in name resolution.
[paul@RHEL5 ~]$ export http_proxy=http://192.168.1.39:8080
[paul@RHEL5 ~]$ wget http://grep.be
--14:35:49--  http://grep.be/
```

```
Connecting to 192.168.1.39:8080... connected.
Proxy request sent, awaiting response... 200 OK
Length: 5390 (5.3K) [text/html]
Saving to: `index.html.1'

100%[================================>] 5,390        --.-K/s    in 0.1s

14:38:29 (54.8 KB/s) - `index.html' saved [5390/5390]

[paul@RHEL5 ~]$
```

Part II. mysql database

Table of Contents

Chapter 3. introduction to sql using mysql

mysql is a database server that understands Structured Query Language (**SQL**). MySQL was developed by the Swedish Company **MySQL AB**. The first release was in 1995. In 2008 MySQL AB was bought by Sun Microsystems (which is now owned by Oracle).

mysql is very popular for websites in combination with **php** and **apache** (the **m** in **lamp** servers), but **mysql** is also used in organizations with huge databases like Facebook, Flickr, Google, Nokia, Wikipedia and Youtube.

This chapter will teach you **sql** by creating and using small databases, tables, queries and a simple trigger in a local **mysql** server.

3.1. installing mysql

On Debian/Ubuntu you can use **aptitude install mysql-server** to install the **mysql server** and **client**.

```
root@ubu1204~# aptitude install mysql-server
The following NEW packages will be installed:
  libdbd-mysql-perl{a} libdbi-perl{a} libhtml-template-perl{a}
  libnet-daemon-perl{a} libplrpc-perl{a} mysql-client-5.5{a}
  mysql-client-core-5.5{a} mysql-server mysql-server-5.5{a}
  mysql-server-core-5.5{a}
0 packages upgraded, 10 newly installed, 0 to remove and 1 not upgraded.
Need to get 25.5 MB of archives. After unpacking 88.4 MB will be used.
Do you want to continue? [Y/n/?]
```

During the installation you will be asked to provide a password for the **root mysql user**, remember this password (or use **hunter2** like i do.

To verify the installed version, use **dpkg -l** on Debian/Ubuntu. This screenshot shows version 5.0 installed.

```
root@ubu1204~# dpkg -l mysql-server | tail -1 | tr -s ' ' | cut -c-72
ii mysql-server 5.5.24-0ubuntu0.12.04.1 MySQL database server (metapacka
```

Issue **rpm -q** to get version information about MySQL on Red Hat/Fedora/CentOS.

```
[paul@RHEL52 ~]$ rpm -q mysql-server
mysql-server-5.0.45-7.el5
```

You will need at least version 5.0 to work with **triggers**.

3.2. accessing mysql

3.2.1. Linux users

The installation of **mysql** creates a user account in **/etc/passwd** and a group account in **/etc/group**.

```
kevin@ubu1204:~$ tail -1 /etc/passwd
mysql:x:120:131:MySQL Server,,,:/nonexistent:/bin/false
kevin@ubu1204:~$ tail -1 /etc/group
mysql:x:131:
```

The mysql daemon **mysqld** will run with the credentials of this user and group.

```
root@ubu1204~# ps -eo uid,user,gid,group,comm | grep mysqld
  120 mysql        131 mysql     mysqld
```

3.2.2. mysql client application

You can now use mysql from the commandline by just typing **mysql -u root -p** and you 'll be asked for the password (of the **mysql root** account). In the screenshot below the user typed **exit** to exit the mysql console.

```
root@ubu1204~# mysql -u root -p
Enter password:
Welcome to the MySQL monitor.  Commands end with ; or \g.
Your MySQL connection id is 43
Server version: 5.5.24-0ubuntu0.12.04.1 (Ubuntu)

Copyright (c) 2000, 2011, Oracle and/or its affiliates. All rights reserved.

Oracle is a registered trademark of Oracle Corporation and/or its
affiliates. Other names may be trademarks of their respective
owners.

Type 'help;' or '\h' for help. Type '\c' to clear the current input statement.

mysql> exit
Bye
```

You could also put the password in clear text on the command line, but that would not be very secure. Anyone with access to your bash history would be able to read your mysql root password.

```
root@ubu1204~# mysql -u root -phunter2
Welcome to the MySQL monitor.  Commands end with ; or \g.
...
```

3.2.3. ~/.my.cnf

You can save configuration in your home directory in the hidden file **.my.cnf**. In the screenshot below we put the root user and password in .my.cnf.

```
kevin@ubu1204:~$ pwd
/home/kevin
kevin@ubu1204:~$ cat .my.cnf
[client]
user=root
password=hunter2
kevin@ubu1204:~$
```

This enables us to log on as the **root mysql** user just by typing **mysql**.

```
kevin@ubu1204:~$ mysql
Welcome to the MySQL monitor.  Commands end with ; or \g.
Your MySQL connection id is 56
Server version: 5.5.24-0ubuntu0.12.04.1 (Ubuntu)
```

3.2.4. the mysql command line client

You can use the **mysql** command to take a look at the databases, and to execute SQL queries on them. The screenshots below show you how.

Here we execute the command **show databases**. Every command must be terminated by a delimiter. The default delimiter is **;** (the semicolon).

```
mysql> show databases;
+--------------------+
| Database           |
+--------------------+
| information_schema |
| mysql              |
| performance_schema |
| test               |
+--------------------+
4 rows in set (0.00 sec)
```

We will use this prompt in the next sections.

3.3. mysql databases

3.3.1. listing all databases

You can use the **mysql** command to take a look at the databases, and to execute SQL queries on them. The screenshots below show you how. First, we log on to our MySQL server and execute the command **show databases** to see which databases exist on our mysql server.

```
kevin@ubu1204:~$ mysql
Welcome to the MySQL monitor.  Commands end with ; or \g.
Your MySQL connection id is 57
Server version: 5.5.24-0ubuntu0.12.04.1 (Ubuntu)

Copyright (c) 2000, 2011, Oracle and/or its affiliates. All rights reserved.

Oracle is a registered trademark of Oracle Corporation and/or its
affiliates. Other names may be trademarks of their respective
owners.

Type 'help;' or '\h' for help. Type '\c' to clear the current input statement.

mysql> show databases;
+--------------------+
| Database           |
+--------------------+
| information_schema |
| mysql              |
| performance_schema |
| test               |
+--------------------+
4 rows in set (0.00 sec)
```

3.3.2. creating a database

You can create a new database with the **create database** command.

```
mysql> create database famouspeople;
Query OK, 1 row affected (0.00 sec)

mysql> show databases;
+--------------------+
| Database           |
+--------------------+
| information_schema |
| famouspeople       |
| mysql              |
| performance_schema |
| test               |
+--------------------+
5 rows in set (0.00 sec)
```

47

3.3.3. using a database

Next we tell **mysql** to use one particular database with the **use $database** command. This screenshot shows how to make wikidb the current database (in use).

```
mysql> use famouspeople;
Database changed
mysql>
```

3.3.4. access to a database

To give someone access to a mysql database, use the **grant** command.

```
mysql> grant all on famouspeople.* to kevin@localhost IDENTIFIED BY "hunter2";
Query OK, 0 rows affected (0.00 sec)
```

3.3.5. deleting a database

When a database is no longer needed, you can permanently remove it with the **drop database** command.

```
mysql> drop database demodb;
Query OK, 1 row affected (0.09 sec)
```

3.3.6. backup and restore a database

You can take a backup of a database, or move it to another computer using the **mysql** and **mysqldump** commands. In the screenshot below, we take a backup of the wikidb database on the computer named laika.

```
mysqldump -u root famouspeople > famouspeople.backup.20120708.sql
```

Here is a screenshot of a database restore operation from this backup.

```
mysql -u root famouspeople < famouspeople.backup.20120708.sql
```

3.4. mysql tables

3.4.1. listing tables

You can see a list of tables in the current database with the **show tables;** command. Our **famouspeople** database has no tables yet.

```
mysql> use famouspeople;
Database changed
mysql> show tables;
Empty set (0.00 sec)
```

3.4.2. creating a table

The **create table** command will create a new table.

This screenshot shows the creation of a country table. We use the **countrycode** as a **primary key** (all country codes are uniquely defined). Most country codes are two or three letters, so a **char** of three uses less space than a **varchar** of three. The **country name** and the name of the capital are both defined as **varchar**. The population can be seen as an **integer**.

```
mysql> create table country (
    -> countrycode char(3) NOT NULL,
    -> countryname varchar(70) NOT NULL,
    -> population int,
    -> countrycapital varchar(50),
    -> primary key (countrycode)
    -> );
Query OK, 0 rows affected (0.19 sec)

mysql> show tables;
+-----------------------+
| Tables_in_famouspeople |
+-----------------------+
| country               |
+-----------------------+
1 row in set (0.00 sec)

mysql>
```

You are allowed to type the **create table** command on one long line, but administrators often use multiple lines to improve readability.

```
mysql> create table country ( countrycode char(3) NOT NULL, countryname\
 varchar(70) NOT NULL, population int, countrycapital varchar(50), prim\
ary key (countrycode) );
Query OK, 0 rows affected (0.18 sec)
```

3.4.3. describing a table

To see a description of the structure of a table, issue the **describe $tablename** command as shown below.

```
mysql> describe country;
+---------------+-------------+------+-----+---------+-------+
| Field         | Type        | Null | Key | Default | Extra |
+---------------+-------------+------+-----+---------+-------+
| countrycode   | char(3)     | NO   | PRI | NULL    |       |
| countryname   | varchar(70) | NO   |     | NULL    |       |
| population    | int(11)     | YES  |     | NULL    |       |
| countrycapital| varchar(50) | YES  |     | NULL    |       |
+---------------+-------------+------+-----+---------+-------+
4 rows in set (0.00 sec)
```

3.4.4. removing a table

To remove a table from a database, issue the **drop table $tablename** command as shown below.

```
mysql> drop table country;
Query OK, 0 rows affected (0.00 sec)
```

3.5. mysql records

3.5.1. creating records

Use **insert** to enter data into the table. The screenshot shows several insert statements that insert values depending on the position of the data in the statement.

```
mysql> insert into country values ('BE','Belgium','11000000','Brussels');
Query OK, 1 row affected (0.05 sec)

mysql> insert into country values ('DE','Germany','82000000','Berlin');
Query OK, 1 row affected (0.05 sec)

mysql> insert into country values ('JP','Japan','128000000','Tokyo');
Query OK, 1 row affected (0.05 sec)
```

Some administrators prefer to use uppercase for **sql** keywords. The mysql client accepts both.

```
mysql> INSERT INTO country VALUES ('FR','France','64000000','Paris');
Query OK, 1 row affected (0.00 sec)
```

Note that you get an error when using a duplicate **primary key**.

```
mysql> insert into country values ('DE','Germany','82000000','Berlin');
ERROR 1062 (23000): Duplicate entry 'DE' for key 'PRIMARY'
```

3.5.2. viewing all records

Below an example of a simple **select** query to look at the contents of a table.

```
mysql> select * from country;
+-------------+---------------+------------+---------------+
| countrycode | countryname   | population | countrycapital|
+-------------+---------------+------------+---------------+
| BE          | Belgium       |   11000000 | Brussels      |
| CN          | China         | 1400000000 | Beijing       |
| DE          | Germany       |   82000000 | Berlin        |
| FR          | France        |   64000000 | Paris         |
| IN          | India         | 1300000000 | New Delhi     |
| JP          | Japan         |  128000000 | Tokyo         |
| MX          | Mexico        |  113000000 | Mexico City   |
| US          | United States |  313000000 | Washington    |
+-------------+---------------+------------+---------------+
8 rows in set (0.00 sec)
```

3.5.3. updating records

Consider the following **insert** statement. The capital of Spain is not Barcelona, it is Madrid.

```
mysql> insert into country values ('ES','Spain','48000000','Barcelona');
Query OK, 1 row affected (0.08 sec)
```

Using an **update** statement, the record can be updated.

```
mysql> update country set countrycapital='Madrid' where countrycode='ES';
Query OK, 1 row affected (0.07 sec)
Rows matched: 1  Changed: 1  Warnings: 0
```

We can use a **select** statement to verify this change.

```
mysql> select * from country;
+-------------+---------------+------------+---------------+
| countrycode | countryname   | population | countrycapital |
+-------------+---------------+------------+---------------+
| BE          | Belgium       |   11000000 | Brussels      |
| CN          | China         | 1400000000 | Beijing       |
| DE          | Germany       |   82000000 | Berlin        |
| ES          | Spain         |   48000000 | Madrid        |
| FR          | France        |   64000000 | Paris         |
| IN          | India         | 1300000000 | New Delhi     |
| JP          | Japan         |  128000000 | Tokyo         |
| MX          | Mexico        |  113000000 | Mexico City   |
| US          | United States |  313000000 | Washington    |
+-------------+---------------+------------+---------------+
9 rows in set (0.00 sec)
```

3.5.4. viewing selected records

Using a **where** clause in a **select** statement, you can specify which record(s) you want to see.

```
mysql> SELECT * FROM country WHERE countrycode='ES';
+-------------+-------------+------------+---------------+
| countrycode | countryname | population | countrycapital |
+-------------+-------------+------------+---------------+
| ES          | Spain       |   48000000 | Madrid        |
+-------------+-------------+------------+---------------+
1 row in set (0.00 sec)
```

Another example of the **where** clause.

```
mysql> select * from country where countryname='Spain';
+-------------+-------------+------------+---------------+
| countrycode | countryname | population | countrycapital |
+-------------+-------------+------------+---------------+
| ES          | Spain       |   48000000 | Madrid        |
+-------------+-------------+------------+---------------+
1 row in set (0.00 sec)
```

3.5.5. primary key in where clause ?

The **primary key** of a table is a field that uniquely identifies every record (every row) in the table. when using another field in the **where** clause, it is possible to get multiple rows returned.

```
mysql> insert into country values ('EG','Egypt','82000000','Cairo');
```

```
Query OK, 1 row affected (0.33 sec)

mysql> select * from country where population='82000000';
+-------------+-------------+------------+----------------+
| countrycode | countryname | population | countrycapital |
+-------------+-------------+------------+----------------+
| DE          | Germany     |   82000000 | Berlin         |
| EG          | Egypt       |   82000000 | Cairo          |
+-------------+-------------+------------+----------------+
2 rows in set (0.00 sec)
```

3.5.6. ordering records

We know that **select** allows us to see all records in a table. Consider this table.

```
mysql> select countryname,population from country;
+---------------+------------+
| countryname   | population |
+---------------+------------+
| Belgium       |   11000000 |
| China         | 1400000000 |
| Germany       |   82000000 |
| Egypt         |   82000000 |
| Spain         |   48000000 |
| France        |   64000000 |
| India         | 1300000000 |
| Japan         |  128000000 |
| Mexico        |  113000000 |
| United States |  313000000 |
+---------------+------------+
10 rows in set (0.00 sec)
```

Using the **order by** clause, we can change the order in which the records are presented.

```
mysql> select countryname,population from country order by countryname;
+---------------+------------+
| countryname   | population |
+---------------+------------+
| Belgium       |   11000000 |
| China         | 1400000000 |
| Egypt         |   82000000 |
| France        |   64000000 |
| Germany       |   82000000 |
| India         | 1300000000 |
| Japan         |  128000000 |
| Mexico        |  113000000 |
| Spain         |   48000000 |
| United States |  313000000 |
+---------------+------------+
10 rows in set (0.00 sec)
```

3.5.7. grouping records

Consider this table of people. The screenshot shows how to use the **avg** function to calculate an average.

```
mysql> select * from people;
+---------------+----------+-----------+-------------+
| Name          | Field    | birthyear | countrycode |
+---------------+----------+-----------+-------------+
| Barack Obama  | politics | 1961      | US          |
| Deng Xiaoping | politics | 1904      | CN          |
```

```
| Guy Verhofstadt | politics   | 1953 | BE |          |
| Justine Henin   | tennis     | 1982 | BE |          |
| Kim Clijsters   | tennis     | 1983 | BE |          |
| Li Na           | tennis     | 1982 | CN |          |
| Liu Yang        | astronaut  | 1978 | CN |          |
| Serena Williams | tennis     | 1981 | US |          |
| Venus Williams  | tennis     | 1980 | US |          |
+-----------------+------------+------+----+----------+
9 rows in set (0.00 sec)

mysql> select Field,AVG(birthyear) from people;
+----------+-------------------+
| Field    | AVG(birthyear)    |
+----------+-------------------+
| politics | 1967.111111111111 |
+----------+-------------------+
1 row in set (0.00 sec)
```

Using the **group by** clause, we can have an average per field.

```
mysql> select Field,AVG(birthyear) from people group by Field;
+----------+-------------------+
| Field    | AVG(birthyear)    |
+----------+-------------------+
| astronaut |             1978 |
| politics  | 1939.3333333333333 |
| tennis    |           1981.6 |
+----------+-------------------+
3 rows in set (0.00 sec)
```

3.5.8. deleting records

You can use the **delete** to permanently remove a record from a table.

```
mysql> delete from country where countryname='Spain';
Query OK, 1 row affected (0.06 sec)

mysql> select * from country where countryname='Spain';
Empty set (0.00 sec)
```

3.6. joining two tables

3.6.1. inner join

With an **inner join** you can take values from two tables and combine them in one result. Consider the country and the people tables from the previous section when looking at this screenshot of an **inner join**.

```
mysql> select Name,Field,countryname
    -> from country
    -> inner join people on people.countrycode=country.countrycode;
+-----------------+----------+---------------+
| Name            | Field    | countryname   |
+-----------------+----------+---------------+
| Barack Obama    | politics | United States |
| Deng Xiaoping   | politics | China         |
| Guy Verhofstadt | politics | Belgium       |
| Justine Henin   | tennis   | Belgium       |
| Kim Clijsters   | tennis   | Belgium       |
| Li Na           | tennis   | China         |
```

```
| Liu Yang         | astronaut | China         |
| Serena Williams  | tennis    | United States |
| Venus Williams   | tennis    | United States |
+------------------+-----------+---------------+
9 rows in set (0.00 sec)
```

This **inner join** will show only records with a match on **countrycode** in both tables.

3.6.2. left join

A **left join** is different from an **inner join** in that it will take all rows from the left table, regardless of a match in the right table.

```
mysql> select Name,Field,countryname from country left join people on people.countrycode=count
+------------------+-----------+---------------+
| Name             | Field     | countryname   |
+------------------+-----------+---------------+
| Guy Verhofstadt  | politics  | Belgium       |
| Justine Henin    | tennis    | Belgium       |
| Kim Clijsters    | tennis    | Belgium       |
| Deng Xiaoping    | politics  | China         |
| Li Na            | tennis    | China         |
| Liu Yang         | astronaut | China         |
| NULL             | NULL      | Germany       |
| NULL             | NULL      | Egypt         |
| NULL             | NULL      | Spain         |
| NULL             | NULL      | France        |
| NULL             | NULL      | India         |
| NULL             | NULL      | Japan         |
| NULL             | NULL      | Mexico        |
| Barack Obama     | politics  | United States |
| Serena Williams  | tennis    | United States |
| Venus Williams   | tennis    | United States |
+------------------+-----------+---------------+
16 rows in set (0.00 sec)
```

You can see that some countries are present, even when they have no matching records in the **people** table.

3.7. mysql triggers

3.7.1. using a before trigger

Consider the following **create table** command. The last field (**amount**) is the multiplication of the two fields named **unitprice** and **unitcount**.

```
mysql> create table invoices (
    -> id char(8) NOT NULL,
    -> customerid char(3) NOT NULL,
    -> unitprice int,
    -> unitcount smallint,
    -> amount int );
Query OK, 0 rows affected (0.00 sec)
```

We can let mysql do the calculation for that by using a **before trigger**. The screenshot below shows the creation of a trigger that calculates the amount by multiplying two fields that are about to be inserted.

```
mysql> create trigger total_amount before INSERT on invoices
```

```
    -> for each row set new.amount = new.unitprice * new.unitcount ;
Query OK, 0 rows affected (0.02 sec)
```

Here we verify that the trigger works by inserting a new record, without providing the total amount.

```
mysql> insert into invoices values ('20090526','ABC','199','10','');
Query OK, 1 row affected (0.02 sec)
```

Looking at the record proves that the trigger works.

```
mysql> select * from invoices;
+----------+------------+-----------+-----------+--------+
| id       | customerid | unitprice | unitcount | amount |
+----------+------------+-----------+-----------+--------+
| 20090526 | ABC        |       199 |        10 |   1990 |
+----------+------------+-----------+-----------+--------+
1 row in set (0.00 sec)
```

3.7.2. removing a trigger

When a **trigger** is no longer needed, you can delete it with the **drop trigger** command.

```
mysql> drop trigger total_amount;
Query OK, 0 rows affected (0.00 sec)
```

Part III. dns server

Table of Contents

Chapter 4. introduction to DNS

dns is a fundamental part of every large computer network. **dns** is used by many network services to translate names into network addresses and to locate services on the network (by name).

Whenever you visit a web site, send an e-mail, log on to Active Directory, play Minecraft, chat, or use VoIP, there will be one or (many) more queries to **dns** services.

Should **dns** fail at your organization, then the whole network will grind to a halt (unless you hardcoded the network addresses).

You will notice that even the largest of organizations benefit greatly from having one **dns** infrastructure. Thus **dns** requires all business units to work together.

Even at home, most home modems and routers have builtin **dns** functionality.

This module will explain what **dns** actually is and how to set it up using **Linux** and **bind9**.

4.1. about dns

4.1.1. name to ip address resolution

The **domain name system** or **dns** is a service on a tcp/ip network that enables clients to translate names into ip addresses. Actually **dns** is much more than that, but let's keep it simple for now.

When you use a browser to go to a website, then you type the name of that website in the url bar. But for your computer to actually communicate with the web server hosting said website, your computer needs the ip address of that web server. That is where **dns** comes in.

In wireshark you can use the **dns** filter to see this traffic.

No..	Time	Source	Destination	Protocol	Info
4560	11.467767	192.168.1.30	212.71.8.10	DNS	Standard query A google.com
4569	11.487774	212.71.8.10	192.168.1.30	DNS	Standard query response A 66.102.13.105

Filter: dns   Expression... Clear Apply

4.1.2. history

In the Seventies, only a few hundred computers were connected to the internet. To resolve names, computers had a flat file that contained a table to resolve hostnames to ip addresses. This local file was downloaded from **hosts.txt** on an ftp server in Stanford.

In 1984 **Paul Mockapetris** created **dns**, a distributed treelike hierarchical database that will be explained in detail in these chapters.

Today, **dns** or **domain name system** is a worldwide distributed hierarchical database controlled by **ICANN**. Its primary function is to resolve names to ip addresses, and to point to internet servers providing **smtp** or **ldap** services.

The old **hosts.txt** file is still active today on most computer systems under the name **/etc/hosts** (or C:/Windows/System32/Drivers/etc/hosts). We will discuss this file later, as it can influence name resolution.

4.1.3. forward and reverse lookup queries

The question a client asks a dns server is called a **query**. When a client queries for an ip address, this is called a **forward lookup query** (as seen in the previous drawing).

The reverse, a query for the name of a host, is called a **reverse lookup query**.

Below a picture of a **reverse lookup query**.

Who is 178.63.30.100 ?

It is antares.ginsys.net.

192.168.1.30

212.71.8.10

Here is a screenshot of a **reverse lookup query** in **nslookup**.

```
root@debian7:~# nslookup
> set type=PTR
> 188.93.155.87
Server:         192.168.1.42
Address:        192.168.1.42#53

Non-authoritative answer:
87.155.93.188.in-addr.arpa      name = antares.ginsys.net.
```

This is what a reverse lookup looks like when sniffing with **tcpdump**.

```
root@debian7:~# tcpdump udp port 53
tcpdump: verbose output suppressed, use -v or -vv for full protocol decode
listening on eth0, link-type EN10MB (Ethernet), capture size 65535 bytes
11:01:29.357685 IP 192.168.1.103.42041 > 192.168.1.42.domain: 14763+ PT\
R? 87.155.93.188.in-addr.arpa. (44)
11:01:29.640093 IP 192.168.1.42.domain > 192.168.1.103.42041: 14763 1/0\
/0 PTR antares.ginsys.net. (76)
```

And here is what it looks like in **wireshark** (note this is an older screenshot).

Filter:	dns				Expression... Clear Apply
No. ▴	Time	Source	Destination	Protocol	Info
280	172.307847	192.168.1.30	212.71.8.10	DNS	Standard query PTR 100.30.63.178.in-addr.arpa
281	172.321299	212.71.8.10	192.168.1.30	DNS	Standard query response PTR antares.ginsys.net

4.1.4. /etc/resolv.conf

A client computer needs to know the ip address of the **dns server** to be able to send queries to it. This is either provided by a **dhcp server** or manually entered.

Linux clients keep this information in the **/etc/resolv.conf** file.

```
root@debian7:~# cat /etc/resolv.conf
domain linux-training.be
search linux-training.be
nameserver 192.168.1.42
root@debian7:~#
```

You can manually change the ip address in this file to use another **dns** server. For example Google provides a public name server at 8.8.8.8 and 8.8.4.4.

```
root@debian7:~# cat /etc/resolv.conf
nameserver 8.8.8.8
root@debian7:~#
```

Please note that on **dhcp clients** this value can be overwritten when the **dhcp lease** is renewed.

4.2. dns namespace

4.2.1. hierarchy

The **dns namespace** is hierarchical tree structure, with the **root servers** (aka dot-servers) at the top. The **root servers** are usually represented by a dot.

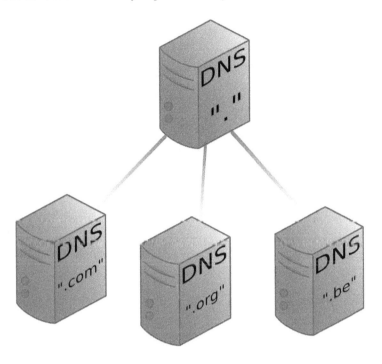

Below the **root-servers** are the **Top Level Domains** or **tld**'s.

There are more **tld**'s than shown in the picture. Currently about 200 countries have a **tld**. And there are several general **tld**'s like .com, .edu, .org, .gov, .net, .mil, .int and more recently also .aero, .info, .museum, ...

4.2.2. root servers

There are thirteen **root servers** on the internet, they are named **A** to **M**. Journalists often refer to these servers as **the master servers of the internet**, because if these servers go down, then nobody can (use names to) connect to websites.

The root servers are not thirteen physical machines, they are many more. For example the **F** root server consists of 46 physical machines that all behave as one (using anycast).

```
http://root-servers.org
http://f.root-servers.org
http://en.wikipedia.org/wiki/Root_nameserver.
```

4.2.3. root hints

Every **dns server software** will come with a list of **root hints** to locate the **root servers**.

This screenshot shows a small portion of the root hints file that comes with **bind 9.8.4**.

```
root@debian7:~# grep -w 'A ' /etc/bind/db.root
A.ROOT-SERVERS.NET.        3600000        A        198.41.0.4
B.ROOT-SERVERS.NET.        3600000        A        192.228.79.201
C.ROOT-SERVERS.NET.        3600000        A        192.33.4.12
D.ROOT-SERVERS.NET.        3600000        A        199.7.91.13
E.ROOT-SERVERS.NET.        3600000        A        192.203.230.10
F.ROOT-SERVERS.NET.        3600000        A        192.5.5.241
G.ROOT-SERVERS.NET.        3600000        A        192.112.36.4
H.ROOT-SERVERS.NET.        3600000        A        128.63.2.53
I.ROOT-SERVERS.NET.        3600000        A        192.36.148.17
J.ROOT-SERVERS.NET.        3600000        A        192.58.128.30
K.ROOT-SERVERS.NET.        3600000        A        193.0.14.129
L.ROOT-SERVERS.NET.        3600000        A        199.7.83.42
M.ROOT-SERVERS.NET.        3600000        A        202.12.27.33
root@debian7:~#
```

4.2.4. domains

One level below the **top level domains** are the **domains**. Domains can have subdomains (also called child domains).

This picture shows **dns domains** like google.com, chess.com, linux-training.be (there are millions more).

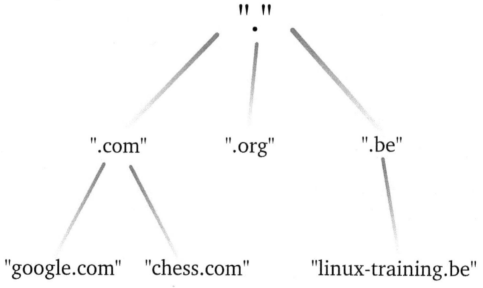

DNS domains are registered at the **tld** servers, the **tld** servers are registered at the **dot servers**.

4.2.5. top level domains

Below the root level are the **top level domains** or **tld's**. Originally there were only seven defined:

Table 4.1. the first top level domains

year	TLD	purpose
1985	.arpa	Reverse lookup via in-addr.arpa
1985	.com	Commercial Organizations
1985	.edu	US Educational Institutions
1985	.gov	US Government Institutions
1985	.mil	US Military
1985	.net	Internet Service Providers, Internet Infrastructure
1985	.org	Non profit Organizations
1988	.int	International Treaties like nato.int

Country **tld**'s were defined for individual countries, like **.uk** in 1985 for Great Britain (yes really), **.be** for Belgium in 1988 and **.fr** for France in 1986. See RFC 1591 for more info.

In 1998 seven new general purpose **tld**'s where chosen, they became active in the 21st century.

Table 4.2. new general purpose tld's

year	TLD	purpose
2002	.aero	aviation related
2001	.biz	businesses
2001	.coop	for co-operatives
2001	.info	informative internet resources
2001	.museum	for museums
2001	.name	for all kinds of names, pseudonyms and labels...
2004	.pro	for professionals

Many people were surprised by the choices, claiming not much use for them and wanting a separate **.xxx** domain (introduced in 2011) for adult content, and **.kidz** a save haven for children. In the meantime more useless **tld**'s were create like **.travel** (for travel agents) and **.tel** (for internet communications) and **.jobs** (for jobs sites).

In 2012 **ICANN** released a list of 2000 new **tld**'s that would gradually become available.

4.2.6. fully qualified domain name

The **fully qualified domain name** or **fqdn** is the combination of the **hostname** of a machine appended with its **domain name**.

If for example a system is called **gwen** and it is in the domain **linux-training.be**, then the fqdn of this system is **gwen.linux-training.be**.

On Linux systems you can use the **hostname** and **dnsdomainname** commands to verify this information.

```
root@gwen:~# hostname
gwen
root@gwen:~# dnsdomainname
linux-training.be
root@gwen:~# hostname --fqdn
gwen.linux-training.be
root@gwen:~# cat /etc/debian_version
6.0.10
```

4.2.7. dns zones

A **zone** (aka a **zone of authority**) is a portion of the DNS tree that covers one domain name or child domain name. The picture below represents zones as blue ovals. Some zones will contain delegate authority over a child domain to another zone.

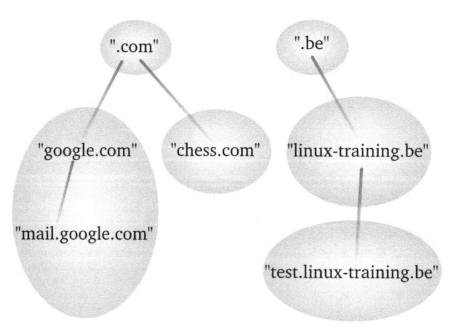

A **dns server** can be **authoritative** over 0, 1 or more **dns zones**. We will see more details later on the relation between a **dns server** and a **dns zone**.

A **dns zone** consists of **records**, also called **resource records**. We will list some of those **resource records** on the next page.

4.2.8. dns records

A record

The **A record**, which is also called a **host record** contains the ipv4-address of a computer. When a DNS client queries a DNS server for an A record, then the DNS server will resolve the hostname in the query to an ip address. An **AAAA record** is similar but contains an ipv6 address instead of ipv4.

PTR record

A **PTR record** is the reverse of an A record. It contains the name of a computer and can be used to resolve an ip address to a hostname.

NS record

A **NS record** or **nameserver record** is a record that points to a DNS name server (in this zone). You can list all your name servers for your DNS zone in distinct NS records.

glue A record

An A record that maps the name of an NS record to an ip address is said to be a **glue record**.

SOA record

The SOA record of a zone contains meta information about the zone itself. The contents of the SOA record is explained in detail in the section about zone transfers. There is exactly one SOA record for each zone.

CNAME record

A **CNAME record** maps a hostname to a hostname, creating effectively an alias for an existing hostname. The name of the mail server is often aliased to **mail** or **smtp**, and the name of a web server to **www**.

MX record

The **MX** record points to an **smtp server**. When you send an email to another domain, then your mail server will need the MX record of the target domain's mail server.

4.3. caching only servers

A **dns server** that is set up without **authority** over a **zone**, but that is connected to other name servers and caches the queries is called a **caching only name server**. Caching only name servers do not have a **zone database** with resource records. Instead they connect to other name servers and cache that information.

There are two kinds of caching only name servers. Those with a **forwarder**, and those that use the **root servers**.

4.3.1. caching only server without forwarder

A caching only server without forwarder will have to get information elsewhere. When it receives a query from a client, then it will consult one of the **root servers**. The **root server** will refer it to a **tld** server, which will refer it to another **dns** server. That last server might know the answer to the query, or may refer to yet another server. In the end, our hard working **dns** server will find an answer and report this back to the client.

In the picture below, the clients asks for the ip address of linux-training.be. Our caching only server will contact the root server, and be refered to the .be server. It will then contact the .be server and be refered to one of the name servers of Openminds. One of these name servers (in this cas ns1.openminds.be) will answer the query with the ip address of linux-training.be. When our caching only server reports this to the client, then the client can connect to this website.

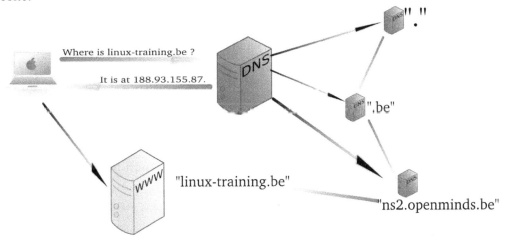

Sniffing with **tcpdump** will give you this (the first 20 characters of each line are cut).

```
192.168.1.103.41251 > M.ROOT-SERVERS.NET.domain: 37279% [1au] A? linux-tr\
aining.be. (46)
M.ROOT-SERVERS.NET.domain > 192.168.1.103.41251: 37279- 0/11/13 (740)
192.168.1.103.65268 > d.ns.dns.be.domain: 38555% [1au] A? linux-training.\
be. (46)
d.ns.dns.be.domain > 192.168.1.103.65268: 38555- 0/7/5 (737)
192.168.1.103.7514 > ns2.openminds.be.domain: 60888% [1au] A? linux-train\
ing.be. (46)
ns2.openminds.be.domain > 192.168.1.103.7514: 60888*- 1/0/1 A 188.93.155.\
87 (62)
```

4.3.2. caching only server with forwarder

A **caching only server** with a **forwarder** is a DNS server that will get all its information from the **forwarder**. The **forwarder** must be a **dns server** for example the **dns server** of an **internet service provider**.

This picture shows a **dns server** on the company LAN that has set the **dns server** from their **isp** as a **forwarder**. If the ip address of the **isp dns server** is 212.71.8.10, then the following lines would occur in the **named.conf** file of the company **dns server**:

```
forwarders {
  212.71.8.10;
};
```

You can also configure your **dns server** to work with **conditional forwarder(s)**. The definition of a conditional forwarder looks like this.

```
zone "someotherdomain.local" {
        type forward;
        forward only;
        forwarders { 10.104.42.1; };
};
```

4.3.3. iterative or recursive query

A **recursive query** is a DNS query where the client that is submitting the query expects a complete answer (Like the fat red arrow above going from the Macbook to the DNS server). An **iterative query** is a DNS query where the client does not expect a complete answer (the three black arrows originating from the DNS server in the picture above). Iterative queries usually take place between name servers. The root name servers do not respond to recursive queries.

4.4. authoritative dns servers

A DNS server that is controlling a zone, is said to be the **authoritative** DNS server for that zone. Remember that a **zone** is a collection of **resource records**.

4.5. primary and secondary

When you set up the first **authoritative** dns server for a zone, then this is called the **primary dns server**. This server will have a readable and writable copy of the **zone database**. For reasons of fault tolerance, performance or load balancing you may decide to set up another **dns server** with authority over that zone. This is called a **secondary** dns server.

4.6. zone transfers

The slave server receives a copy of the zone database from the master server using a **zone transfer**. Zone transfers are requested by the slave servers at regular intervals. Those intervals are defined in the **soa record**.

You can force a refresh from a zone with **rndc**. The example below force a transfer of the **fred.local** zone, and shows the log from **/var/log/syslog**.

```
root@debian7:/etc/bind# rndc refresh fred.local
```

```
root@debian7:/etc/bind# grep fred /var/log/syslog | tail -7 | cut -c38-
zone fred.local/IN: sending notifies (serial 1)
received control channel command 'refresh fred.local'
zone fred.local/IN: Transfer started.
transfer of 'fred.local/IN' from 10.104.109.1#53: connected using 10.104.33.30#57367
zone fred.local/IN: transferred serial 2
transfer of 'fred.local/IN' from 10.104.109.1#53: Transfer completed: 1 messages, 10 records,
zone fred.local/IN: sending notifies (serial 2)
root@debian7:/etc/bind#
```

4.7. master and slave

When adding a **secondary dns server** to a zone, then you will configure this server as a **slave server** to the **primary server**. The primary server then becomes the **master server** of the slave server.

Often the **primary dns server** is the **master** server of all slaves. Sometimes a **slave server** is **master server** for a second line slave server. In the picture below ns1 is the primary dns server and ns2, ns3 and ns4 are secondaries. The master for slaves ns2 and ns3 is ns1, but the master for ns4 is ns2.

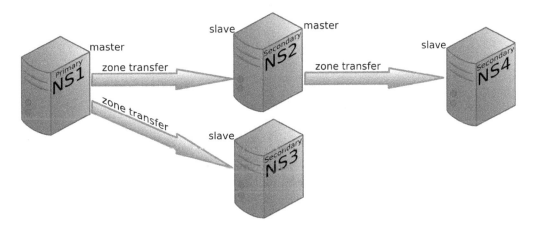

4.8. SOA record

The **soa record** contains a **refresh** value. If this is set to 30 minutes, then the slave server will request a copy of the zone file every 30 minutes. There is also a **retry** value. The retry value is used when the master server did not reply to the last zone transfer request. The value for **expiry time** says how long the slave server will answer to queries, without receiving a zone update.

Below an example of how to use nslookup to query the **soa record** of a zone (linux-training.be).

```
root@debian6:~# nslookup
> set type=SOA
> server ns1.openminds.be
> linux-training.be
Server:         ns1.openminds.be
Address:        195.47.215.14#53

linux-training.be
        origin = ns1.openminds.be
        mail addr = hostmaster.openminds.be
        serial = 2321001133
        refresh = 14400
        retry = 3600
        expire = 604800
        minimum = 3600
```

Zone transfers only occur when the zone database was updated (meaning when one or more resource records were added, removed or changed on the master server). The slave server will compare the **serial number** of its own copy of the SOA record with the serial number of its master's SOA record. When both serial numbers are the same, then no update is needed (because no records were added, removed or deleted). When the slave has a lower serial number than its master, then a zone transfer is requested.

Below a zone transfer captured in wireshark.

	Time	Source	Destination	Protocol	Info
1	0.000000	192.168.1.37	192.168.1.35	DNS	Standard query SOA cobbaut.paul
2	0.008502	192.168.1.35	192.168.1.37	DNS	Standard query response SOA ns.cobbaut.paul
3	0.014672	192.168.1.37	192.168.1.35	TCP	33713 > domain [SYN] Seq=0 Win=5840 Len=0 MS
4	0.015215	192.168.1.35	192.168.1.37	TCP	domain > 33713 [SYN, ACK] Seq=0 Ack=1 Win=57
5	0.015307	192.168.1.37	192.168.1.35	TCP	33713 > domain [ACK] Seq=1 Ack=1 Win=5856 Le
6	0.015954	192.168.1.37	192.168.1.35	TCP	[TCP segment of a reassembled PDU]
7	0.018359	192.168.1.35	192.168.1.37	TCP	domain > 33713 [ACK] Seq=1 Ack=3 Win=5792 Le
8	0.018411	192.168.1.37	192.168.1.35	DNS	Standard query IXFR cobbaut.paul
9	0.018823	192.168.1.35	192.168.1.37	TCP	domain > 33713 [ACK] Seq=1 Ack=77 Win=5792 L
10	0.019784	192.168.1.35	192.168.1.37	DNS	Standard query response SOA ns.cobbaut.paul
11	0.019821	192.168.1.37	192.168.1.35	TCP	33713 > domain [ACK] Seq=77 Ack=295 Win=6912
12	0.020618	192.168.1.37	192.168.1.35	TCP	33713 > domain [FIN, ACK] Seq=77 Ack=295 Win
13	0.021011	192.168.1.35	192.168.1.37	TCP	domain > 33713 [FIN, ACK] Seq=295 Ack=78 Win
14	0.021040	192.168.1.37	192.168.1.35	TCP	33713 > domain [ACK] Seq=78 Ack=296 Win=6912

4.9. full or incremental zone transfers

When a zone tranfer occurs, this can be either a full zone transfer or an incremental zone transfer. The decision depends on the size of the transfer that is needed to completely update the zone on the slave server. An incremental zone transfer is prefered when the total size of changes is smaller than the size of the zone database. Full zone transfers use the **axfr** protocol, incremental zone transfer use the **ixfr** protocol.

4.10. DNS cache

DNS is a caching protocol.

When a client queries its local DNS server, and the local DNS server is not authoritative for the query, then this server will go looking for an authoritative name server in the DNS tree. The local name server will first query a root server, then a **tld** server and then a domain server. When the local name server resolves the query, then it will relay this information to the client that submitted the query, and it will also keep a copy of these queries in its cache. So when a(nother) client submits the same query to this name server, then it will retrieve this information form its cache.

For example, a client queries for the A record on www.linux-training.be to its local server. This is the first query ever received by this local server. The local server checks that it is not authoritative for the linux-training.be domain, nor for the **.be tld**, and it is also not a root server. So the local server will use the root hints to send an **iterative** query to a root server.

The root server will reply with a reference to the server that is authoritative for the .be domain (root DNS servers do not resolve fqdn's, and root servers do not respond to recursive queries).

The local server will then sent an iterative query to the authoritative server for the **.be tld**. This server will respond with a reference to the name server that is authoritative for the linux-training.be domain.

The local server will then sent the query for www.linux-training.be to the authoritative server (or one of its slave servers) for the linux-training.be domain. When the local server receives the ip address for www.linux-training.be, then it will provide this information to the client that submitted this query.

Besides caching the A record for www.linux-training.be, the local server will also cache the NS and A record for the linux-training.be name server and the .be name server.

4.11. forward lookup zone example

The way to set up zones in **/etc/bind/named.conf.local** is to create a zone entry with a reference to another file (this other file contains the **zone database**).

Here is an example of such an entry in **/etc/bind/named.conf.local**:

```
root@debian7:~# cat /etc/bind/named.conf.local
//
// Do any local configuration here
//

// Consider adding the 1918 zones here, if they are not used in your
// organization
//include "/etc/bind/zones.rfc1918";

zone "paul.local" IN {
        type master;
        file "/etc/bind/db.paul.local";
        allow-update { none; };
};
root@debian7:~#
```

To create the zone file, the easy method is to copy an existing zone file (this is easier than writing from scratch).

```
root@debian7:/etc/bind# cp db.empty db.paul.local
root@debian7:/etc/bind# vi db.paul.local
```

Here is an example of a zone file.

```
root@debian7:/etc/bind# cat db.paul.local
; zone for classroom teaching
$TTL    86400
@       IN      SOA     debianpaul.paul.local. root.paul.local (
                        2014100100      ; Serial
                        1h              ; Refresh
                        1h              ; Retry
                        2h              ; Expire
                        86400 )         ; Negative Cache TTL
;
; name servers
;
        IN      NS      ns1
        IN      NS      debianpaul
        IN      NS      debian7
;
; servers
;
debianpaul      IN      A       10.104.33.30
debian7         IN      A       10.104.33.30
ns1             IN      A       10.104.33.30
;www            IN      A       10.104.33.30
```

4.12. example: caching only DNS server

1. installing DNS software on Debian

```
root@debian7:~# aptitude update && aptitude upgrade
...
root@debian7:~# aptitude install bind9
...
root@debian7:~# dpkg -l | grep bind9 | tr -s ' '
ii bind9 1:9.8.4.dfsg.P1-6+nmu2+deb7u2 amd64 Internet Domain Name Server
ii bind9-host 1:9.8.4.dfsg.P1-6+nmu2+deb7u2 amd64 Version of 'host' bundled...
ii bind9utils 1:9.8.4.dfsg.P1-6+nmu2+deb7u2 amd64 Utilities for BIND
ii libbind9-80 1:9.8.4.dfsg.P1-6+nmu2+deb7u2 amd64 BIND9 Shared Library use...
root@debian7:~#
```

2. Discover the default configuration files. Can you define the purpose of each file ?

```
root@debian7:~# ls -l /etc/bind
total 52
-rw-r--r-- 1 root root 2389 Sep  5 20:25 bind.keys
-rw-r--r-- 1 root root  237 Sep  5 20:25 db.0
-rw-r--r-- 1 root root  271 Sep  5 20:25 db.127
-rw-r--r-- 1 root root  237 Sep  5 20:25 db.255
-rw-r--r-- 1 root root  353 Sep  5 20:25 db.empty
-rw-r--r-- 1 root root  270 Sep  5 20:25 db.local
-rw-r--r-- 1 root root 3048 Sep  5 20:25 db.root
-rw-r--r-- 1 root bind  463 Sep  5 20:25 named.conf
-rw-r--r-- 1 root bind  490 Sep  5 20:25 named.conf.default-zones
-rw-r--r-- 1 root bind  374 Oct  1 20:01 named.conf.local
-rw-r--r-- 1 root bind  913 Oct  1 13:24 named.conf.options
-rw-r----- 1 bind bind   77 Oct  1 11:14 rndc.key
-rw-r--r-- 1 root root 1317 Sep  5 20:25 zones.rfc191
```

3. Setup caching only dns server. This is normally the default setup. A caching-only name server will look up names for you and cache them. Many tutorials will tell you to add a **forwarder**, but we first try without this!

Hey this seems to work without a **forwarder**. Using a sniffer you can find out what really happens. Your freshly install dns server is not using a cache, and it is not using your local dns server (from /etc/resolv.conf). So where is this information coming from ? And what can you learn from sniffing this dns traffic ?

4. Explain in detail what happens when you enable a caching only dns server without forwarder. This wireshark screenshot can help, but you learn more by sniffing the traffic yourself.

You should see traffic to a **root name server** whenever you try a new **tld** for the first time. Remember that **dns** is a caching protocol, which means that repeating a query will generate a lot less traffic since your **dns server** will still have the answer in its memory.

4.13. example: caching only with forwarder

5. Add the public Google **dns server** as a **forwarder**. The ip address of this server is 8.8.8.8 .

Before the change:

```
root@debian7:~# grep -A2 'forwarders {' /etc/bind/named.conf.options
        // forwarders {
        //       0.0.0.0;
        // };
```

changing:

```
root@debian7:~# vi /etc/bind/named.conf.options
```

After the change:

```
root@debian7:~# grep -A2 'forwarders {' /etc/bind/named.conf.options
        forwarders {
                8.8.8.8;
        };
```

Restart the server:

```
root@debian7:~# service bind9 restart
Stopping domain name service...: bind9.
Starting domain name service...: bind9.
```

6. Explain the purpose of adding the **forwarder**. What is our **dns server** doing when it receives a query ?

```
root@debian7:~# nslookup
> server
Default server: 10.104.33.30
Address: 10.104.33.30#53
> linux-training.be
Server:         10.104.33.30
Address:        10.104.33.30#53

Non-authoritative answer:
Name:   linux-training.be
Address: 188.93.155.87
>
```

This is the output of **tcpdump udp port 53** while executing the above query for **linux-training.be** in **nslookup**.

```
root@debian7:~# tcpdump udp port 53
tcpdump: verbose output suppressed, use -v or -vv for full protocol decode
listening on eth0, link-type EN10MB (Ethernet), capture size 65535 bytes
```

You should find the following two lines in the output of **tcpdump**:

```
10.104.33.30.19381 > google-public-dns-a.google.com.domain: 18237+% [1au] A? \
linux-training.be. (46)
google-public-dns-a.google.com.domain > 10.104.33.30.19381: 18237 1/0/1 A 188\
.93.155.87 (62)
```

Below is an (old) wireshark screenshot that can help, you should see something similar (but with different ip addresses).

7. What happens when you query for the same domain name more than once ?

8. Why does it say "non-authoritative answer" ? When is a dns server authoritative ?

9. You can also use **dig** instead of **nslookup**.

```
root@debian7:~# dig @10.104.33.30 linux-training.be +short
188.93.155.87
root@debian7:~#
```

10. How can we avoid having to set the server in dig or nslookup ?

Change this:

```
root@debian7:~# cat /etc/resolv.conf
nameserver 10.46.101.1
root@debian7:~#
```

into this:

```
root@debian7:~# cat /etc/resolv.conf
nameserver 10.104.33.30
root@debian7:~#
```

11. When you use **dig** for the first time for a domain, where is the answer coming from ? And the second time ? How can you tell ?

4.14. example: primary authoritative server

1. Instead of only cachng the information from other servers, we will now make our server authoritative for our own domain.

2. I choose the top level domain **.local** and the domain **paul.local** and put the information in **/etc/bind/named.conf.local**.

```
root@debian7:~# cat /etc/bind/named.conf.local
//
// Do any local configuration here
//

// Consider adding the 1918 zones here, if they are not used in your
// organization
//include "/etc/bind/zones.rfc1918";

zone "paul.local" IN {
        type master;
        file "/etc/bind/db.paul.local";
        allow-update { none; };
};
```

3. Also add a **zone database file**, similar to this one (add some A records for testing). Set the **Refresh** and **Retry** values not too high so you can sniff this traffic (this example makes the slave server contact the master every hour).

```
root@debian7:~# cat /etc/bind/db.paul.local
; zone for classroom teaching
$TTL    86400
@       IN      SOA     debianpaul.paul.local. root.paul.local (
                        2014100101      ; Serial
                        1h              ; Refresh
                        1h              ; Retry
                        2h              ; Expire
                        900 )           ; Negative Cache TTL
;
; name servers
;
        IN      NS      ns1
        IN      NS      debianpaul
        IN      NS      debian7
;
; servers
;
debianpaul      IN      A       10.104.33.30
debian7         IN      A       10.104.33.30
ns1             IN      A       10.104.33.30
;www            IN      A       10.104.33.30
root@debian7:~#
```

Note that the **www** record is commented out, so it will not resolve.

4.14.1. using your own DNS server

If you are confident that your **dns server** works, then set it as default and only dns server in **/etc/resolv.conf**.

```
root@debian7:~# cat /etc/resolv.conf
nameserver 10.104.33.30
root@debian7:~#
```

In case you also use **dhclient**, you will need to add your dns server to **/etc/dhcp/ dhclient.conf**.

```
root@debian7:~# diff /etc/dhcp/dhclient.conf /etc/dhcp/dhclient.conf.original
21c21
< prepend domain-name-servers 10.104.33.30;
---
> #prepend domain-name-servers 127.0.0.1;
23,24c23
< #      domain-name, domain-name-servers, domain-search, host-name,
<        domain-name, domain-search, host-name,
---
>        domain-name, domain-name-servers, domain-search, host-name,
root@debian7:~#
```

The above screenshot shows that 10.104.33.30 is now a default option that the **dhcp client** should no longer request from the **dhcp server**.

Adjust **/etc/hosts** to reflect your **domain name** and verify with **hostname** and **dnsdomainname**.

```
root@debian7:~# grep debian7 /etc/hosts
127.0.1.1 debian7.paul.local debian7
root@debian7:~# hostname
debian7
root@debian7:~# hostname --fqdn
debian7.paul.local
root@debian7:~# dnsdomainname
paul.local
```

4.14.2. using your own domain

Consider the following screenshot:

```
root@debian7b:~# cat /etc/resolv.conf
nameserver 10.104.33.30
root@debian7b:~# ping -c1 www
ping: unknown host www
root@debian7b:~# vi /etc/resolv.conf
root@debian7b:~# cat /etc/resolv.conf
nameserver 10.104.33.30
domain paul.local
root@debian7b:~# ping -c1 www
PING www.paul.local (10.104.33.31) 56(84) bytes of data.
64 bytes from 10.104.33.31: icmp_req=1 ttl=64 time=0.021 ms

--- www.paul.local ping statistics ---
1 packets transmitted, 1 received, 0% packet loss, time 0ms
rtt min/avg/max/mdev = 0.021/0.021/0.021/0.000 ms
root@debian7b:~#
```

Adding the **domain paul.local** directive to **/etc/resolv.conf** allows omitting the domain when using hostnames.

You can accomplish this feature automatically by adjusting **dhclient.conf**

```
root@debian7:~# grep paul.local /etc/dhcp/dhclient.conf
prepend domain-name "paul.local";
prepend domain-search "paul.local";
root@debian7:~#
```

4. Restart the DNS server and check your zone in the error log.

```
root@debian7:~# service bind9 restart
Stopping domain name service...: bind9.
Starting domain name service...: bind9.
root@debian7:~# grep paul.local /var/log/syslog
Oct  6 09:22:18 debian7 named[2707]: zone paul.local/IN: loaded seria\
l 2014100101
Oct  6 09:22:18 debian7 named[2707]: zone paul.local/IN: sending noti\
fies (serial 2014100101)
```

5. Use **dig** or **nslookup** (or even **ping**) to test your A records.

```
root@debian7:~# ping -c1 ns1.paul.local
PING ns1.paul.local (10.104.33.30) 56(84) bytes of data.
64 bytes from 10.104.33.30: icmp_req=1 ttl=64 time=0.006 ms

--- ns1.paul.local ping statistics ---
1 packets transmitted, 1 received, 0% packet loss, time 0ms
rtt min/avg/max/mdev = 0.006/0.006/0.006/0.000 ms
root@debian7:~# ping -c1 www.paul.local
ping: unknown host www.paul.local
```

Note that the **www** record was commented out, so it should fail.

```
root@debian7:~# dig debian7.paul.local

; <<>> DiG 9.8.4-rpz2+rl005.12-P1 <<>> debian7.paul.local
;; global options: +cmd
;; Got answer:
;; ->>HEADER<<- opcode: QUERY, status: NOERROR, id: 50491
;; flags: qr aa rd ra; QUERY: 1, ANSWER: 1, AUTHORITY: 3, ADDITIONAL: 2

;; QUESTION SECTION:
;debian7.paul.local.            IN      A

;; ANSWER SECTION:
debian7.paul.local.    86400   IN      A       10.104.33.30

;; AUTHORITY SECTION:
paul.local.            86400   IN      NS      ns1.paul.local.
paul.local.            86400   IN      NS      debian7.paul.local.
paul.local.            86400   IN      NS      debianpaul.paul.local.

;; ADDITIONAL SECTION:
ns1.paul.local.        86400   IN      A       10.104.33.30
debianpaul.paul.local. 86400   IN      A       10.104.33.30

;; Query time: 4 msec
;; SERVER: 10.104.33.30#53(10.104.33.30)
;; WHEN: Mon Oct  6 09:35:25 2014
;; MSG SIZE  rcvd: 141

root@debian7:~#
```

6. Our primary server appears to be up and running. Note the information here:

```
server os  : Debian 7
ip address : 10.104.33.30
domain name: paul.local
server name: ns1.paul.local
```

4.15. example: a DNS slave server

1. A slave server transfers zone information over the network from a master server (a slave can also be a master). A primary server maintains zone records in its local file system. As an exercise, and to verify the work of all students, set up a slave server of all the master servers in the classroom.

2. Before configuring the slave server, we may have to allow transfers from our zone to this server. Remember that this is not very secure since transfers are in clear text and limited to an ip address. This example follows our demo from above.

Imagine a student named **Jesse** having completed the setup as shown before, with the domain name **jesse.local** and the ip address 10.104.15.20. The goal is to have a slave server of paul.local on Jesse's computer and a slave zone of jesse.local on my computer.

Below is an example of an **allow-transfer** statement. Careful, maybe the default allows transfer to any.

```
root@debian7:/etc/bind# cat named.conf.local
//
// Do any local configuration here
//

// Consider adding the 1918 zones here, if they are not used in your
// organization
//include "/etc/bind/zones.rfc1918";

zone "paul.local" IN {
        type master;
        file "/etc/bind/db.paul.local";
        allow-update { none; };
        allow-transfer { 10.104.15.20; };
};
```

3. With the configuration below I can make my server a slave for the **jesse.local** zone.

```
root@debian7:/etc/bind# tail -6 named.conf.local
zone "jesse.local" IN {
        type slave;
        file "/var/cache/named/db.jesse.local";
        masters { 10.104.15.20; };
};

root@debian7:/etc/bind# mkdir /var/cache/named/
root@debian7:/etc/bind# chown bind:bind /var/cache/named/
root@debian7:/etc/bind# ls -ld /var/cache/named/
drwxr-xr-x 2 bind bind 4096 Oct  1 20:01 /var/cache/named/
```

Note that we put the **slave zones** in **/var/cache/named** and not in **/etc/bind**.

4. Restarting bind on the slave server should transfer the zone database file. Verify this in /**var/log/syslog**. (time and date are truncated from the screenshot, and Jesse did not use the current date in the serial number...)

```
root@debian7:/etc/bind# grep jesse /var/log/syslog
named[2731]: zone jesse.local/IN: Transfer started.
named[2731]: transfer of 'jesse.local/IN' from 10.104.15.20#53: connected u\
sing 10.104.33.30#44719
named[2731]: zone jesse.local/IN: transferred serial 20110516
named[2731]: transfer of 'jesse.local/IN' from 10.104.15.20#53: Transfer co\
mpleted: 1 messages, 8 records, 239 bytes, 0.001 secs (239000 bytes/sec)
```

And the contents of the **slave zone**:

```
root@debian7:/etc/bind# cat /var/cache/named/db.jesse.local
$ORIGIN .
$TTL 604800     ; 1 week
jesse.local             IN SOA  ns.jesse.local. root.jesse.local.jesse.local. (
                                20110516   ; serial
                                300        ; refresh (5 minutes)
                                200        ; retry (3 minutes 20 seconds)
                                2419200    ; expire (4 weeks)
                                604800     ; minimum (1 week)
                                )
                        NS      ns.jesse.local.
$ORIGIN jesse.local.
anya                    A       10.104.15.1
mac                     A       10.104.15.30
ns                      A       10.104.15.20
ubu1010srv              A       10.104.15.20
www                     A       10.104.15.25
root@debian7:/etc/bind#
```

4.16. practice: dns

1. Install **bind9** and verify with a sniffer how it works.

2. Add a **forwarder** and verify that it works.

3. Create a **primary forward lookup zone** named yourname.local with at least two NS records and four A records.

4. Use **dig** and **nslookup** to verify your NS and A records.

5. Create a **slave** of your primary zone (on another server) and verify the **zone transfer**.

6. Set up two primary zones on two servers and implement a **conditional forwarder** (you can use the two servers from before).

4.17. solution: dns

1. Install **bind9** and verify with a sniffer how it works.

```
You should see queries to the root name servers with tcpdump or wireshark.
```

2. Add a **forwarder** and verify that it works.

```
The forwarder van be added in named.conf.options as seen in the theory.
```

3. Create a **primary forward lookup zone** named yourname.local with at least two NS records and four A records.

```
This is literally explained in the theory.
```

4. Use **dig** and **nslookup** to verify your NS and A records.

```
This is literally explained in the theory.
```

5. Create a **slave** of your primary zone (on another server) and verify the **zone transfer**.

```
This is literally explained in the theory.
```

6. Set up two primary zones on two servers and implement a **conditional forwarder** (you can use the two servers from before).

```
A conditional forwarder is set in named.conf.local as a zone.
(see the theory on forwarder)
```

Chapter 5. advanced DNS

This chapter expands your DNS server with topics like **round robin dns** for load balancing servers, **dns delegation** to delegate child domains to another team and **split horizon dns** so you can provide local service locations to clients.

There is more to **dns**, content will be added **rsn**.

5.1. example: DNS round robin

When you create multiple A records for the same name, then **bind** will do a **round robin** of the order in which the records are returned. This allows the use of DNS as a load balancer between hosts, since clients will usually take the first ip-address offered.

Consider this example from the **/etc/bind/db.paul.local** zone configuration file. There are two A records for **www** pointing to two distinct ip addresses.

```
root@debian7:~# grep www /etc/bind/db.paul.local
www             IN      A       10.104.33.30
www             IN      A       10.104.33.31
```

Below a screenshot of **nslookup** querying a load balanced A record. Notice the order of ip addresses returned.

```
root@debian7:~# nslookup www.paul.local 10.104.33.30
Server:         10.104.33.30
Address:        10.104.33.30#53

Name:   www.paul.local
Address: 10.104.33.31
Name:   www.paul.local
Address: 10.104.33.30

root@debian7:~# nslookup www.paul.local 10.104.33.30
Server:         10.104.33.30
Address:        10.104.33.30#53

Name:   www.paul.local
Address: 10.104.33.30
Name:   www.paul.local
Address: 10.104.33.31
```

Try to set up a website on two web servers (with a small difference so you can distinguish the websites) and test the **round robin**.

5.2. DNS delegation

You can **delegate** a child domain to another DNS server. The child domain then becomes a new zone, with authority at the new dns server.

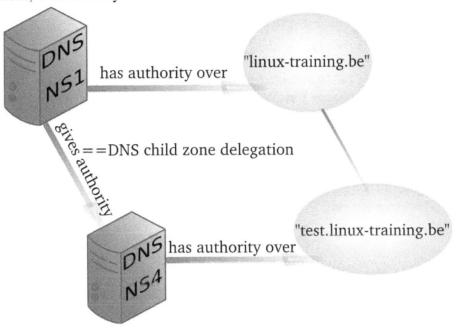

When **delegation** is properly set up, then clients that query your parent zone will also be able to resolve the delegated child zones.

5.3. example: DNS delegation

We have another **Linux server** named **debian7b** and we want to make it responsible for the child domain **test42.paul.local**.

*Note the name of the servers in the screenshots are either **debian7** (hosting the parent domain) or **debian7b** (hosting the child domain).*

We start by adjusting the **/etc/bind/named.comf.local** file (on the server hosting the parent domain) to make sure that no forwarder will be used when resolving authoritative names.

```
root@debian7:~# grep -A4 paul.local /etc/bind/named.conf.local
zone "paul.local" IN {
        type master;
        file "/etc/bind/db.paul.local";
        allow-update { none; };
        allow-transfer { 10.104.15.20; };
        forwarders { };
};
root@debian7:~#
```

Technically, you could also set **allow-transfer** to **{ any; };** while troubleshooting and then refine it later, but this is not needed for delegation.

Then we add the delegation to our zone database:

```
root@debian7:~# tail -3 /etc/bind/db.paul.local
$ORIGIN test42.paul.local.
@       IN      NS      ns2.test42.paul.local.
ns2     IN      A       10.104.33.31    ; the glue record
root@debian7:~#
```

Don't forget to restart **bind** and verify **/var/log/syslog**.

```
root@debian7:~# service bind9 restart
Stopping domain name service...: bind9.
Starting domain name service...: bind9.
root@debian7:~# grep paul.local /var/log/syslog | cut -c28- | tail -2
named[3202]: zone paul.local/IN: loaded serial 2014100801
named[3202]: zone paul.local/IN: sending notifies (serial 2014100801)
root@debian7:~#
```

*Note that on your terminal you can type **tail -40 /var/log/syslog** because the only reason I use **grep**, **cut** and **tail -2** is to limit the size of the screenshots in this book.*

Next we create a zone database file on the second server, as seen in this screenshot:

```
root@debian7b:~# cat /etc/bind/db.test42.paul.local
; child zone for classroom teaching
$TTL    86400
$ORIGIN test42.paul.local.
@       IN      SOA     ns2.test42.paul.local. root.test42.paul.local. (
                        2014100802      ; Serial
                        1h              ; Refresh
                        1h              ; Retry
                        2h              ; Expire
                        900 )           ; Negative Cache TTL
;
; name servers
;
        IN      NS      ns2.test42.paul.local.
        IN      NS      debian7b.test42.paul.local.
;
; servers
;
ns2          IN      A       10.104.33.31
debian7b     IN      A       10.104.33.31
testsrv      IN      A       10.104.33.31
root@debian7b:~#
```

The second server also needs a zone definition in **named.conf.local**, followed by a restart of **bind**.

```
root@debian7b:~# cat /etc/bind/named.conf.local
//
// Do any local configuration here
//

// Consider adding the 1918 zones here, if they are not used in your
// organization
//include "/etc/bind/zones.rfc1918";

zone "test42.paul.local" IN {
        type master;
        file "/etc/bind/db.test42.paul.local";
        allow-update { none; };
        allow-transfer { any; };
};
root@debian7b:~#
```

Testing on the parent server:

```
root@debian7:~# dig ns1.paul.local +short
10.104.33.30
root@debian7:~# dig ns2.test42.paul.local +short
10.104.33.31
root@debian7:~# dig debian7b.test42.paul.local +short
10.104.33.31
```

5.4. example: split-horizon dns

Suppose you want to answer dns queries depending on who is asking. For example when someone from the 10.104.15.0/24 network (managed by Jesse) asks for the A record www.paul.local, then dns answers with 10.104.33.30. But when someone from the 10.104.42.0/24 network (managed by Keith) asks for the same A record of www.paul.local, he will get 10.104.33.31 as an answer.

A **split-horizon** setup can be used to redirect people to **local** copies of certain services.

In this example we want to decide on specific answers for two networks (Jesse's and Keith's) and prevent them from using our dns server for **recursion**, while maintaining the capability to resolve the internet and our paul.local zone from our own network.

We start by creating three **view** clauses in **named.conf.local**.

```
root@debian7:/etc/bind# cat named.conf.local
view "paul" {
match-clients { 10.104.33.0; localhost; };
include "/etc/bind/named.conf.default-zones";
zone "paul.local" IN {
        type master;
        file "/etc/bind/db.paul.local";
        allow-update { none; };
        };
};      // end view internal

view "jesse" {
match-clients { 10.104.15/24; };
zone "paul.local" IN {
        type master;
        file "/etc/bind/db.paul.local.jesse";
        allow-update { none; };
        };
};      // end view jesse

view "keith" {
match-clients { 10.104.42/24; };
zone "paul.local" IN {
        type master;
        file "/etc/bind/db.paul.local.keith";
        allow-update { none; };
        };
};      // end view keith
```

Note that we included the **default-zones** in the internal zone. It is mandatory to put all zones inside views when using a view.

The zone files are identical copies, except for the **www** record. You can see that the **round robin** is still active for internal users, computers from 10.104.15.0/24 (Jesse) will always receive 10.104.33.30 while computers from 10.104.42.0/24 (Keith) will receive 10.104.33.31.

```
root@debian7:/etc/bind# grep www db.paul.local db.paul.local.[jk]*
db.paul.local:www            IN      A       10.104.33.30
db.paul.local:www            IN      A       10.104.33.31
db.paul.local.jesse:www      IN      A       10.104.33.30
db.paul.local.keith:www      IN      A       10.104.33.31
```

5.5. old dns topics

All the dns things below this paragraph are old and in urgent need of review.

5.5.1. old example: reverse DNS

1. We can add ip to name resolution to our dns-server using a reverse dns zone.

2. Start by adding a .arpa zone to /etc/bind/named.conf.local like this (we set notify to no to avoid sending of notify messages to other name servers):

```
root@ubu1010srv:/etc/bind# grep -A4 arpa named.conf.local
zone "1.168.192.in-addr.arpa" {
 type master;
 notify no;
 file "/etc/bind/db.192";
};
```

3. Also create a zone database file for this reverse lookup zone.

```
root@ubu1010srv:/etc/bind# cat db.192
;
; BIND reverse data file for 192.168.1.0/24 network
;
$TTL 604800
@ IN SOA ns.cobbaut.paul root.cobbaut.paul. (
   20110516 ; Serial
    604800   ; Refresh
     86400   ; Retry
   2419200   ; Expire
    604800 ) ; Negative Cache TTL
;
@ IN NS ns.
37 IN PTR ns.cobbaut.paul.
1 IN PTR anya.cobbaut.paul.
30 IN PTR mac.cobbaut.paul.
root@ubu1010srv:/etc/bind#
```

4. Test with nslookup or dig:

```
root@ubu1010srv:/etc/bind# dig 1.168.192.in-addr.arpa AXFR
```

5.5.2. old DNS load balancing

Not as above. When you have more than one DNS server authoritative for a zone, you can spread queries amongst all server. One way to do this is by creating NS records for all servers that participate in the load balancing of external queries.

You could also configure different name servers on internal clients.

5.5.3. old DNS notify

The original design of DNS in rfc 1034 and rfc 1035 implemented a **refresh** time in the **SOA** record to configure a time loop for slaves to query their master server. This can result in a lot of useless pull requests, or in a significant lag between updates.

For this reason **dns notify (rfc 1996)** was designed. The server will now notify slaves whenever there is an update. By default this feature is activated in **bind**.

Notify can be disabled as in this screenshot.

```
zone "1.168.192.in-addr.arpa" {
        type master;
        notify no;
        file "/etc/bind/db.192";
};
```

5.5.4. old testing IXFR and AXFR

Full zone transfers (AXFR) are initiated when you restart the bind server, or when you manually update the zone database file directly. With **nsupdate** you can update a zone database and initiate an incremental zone transfer.

You need DDNS allowed for **nsupdate** to work.

```
root@ubu1010srv:/etc/bind# nsupdate
> server 127.0.0.1
> update add mac14.linux-training.be 86400 A 192.168.1.23
> send
update failed: REFUSED
```

5.5.5. old DDNS integration with DHCP

Some organizations like to have all their client computers in DNS. This can be cumbersome to maintain. Luckily **rfc 2136** describes integration of DHCP servers with a DNS server. Whenever DHCP acknowledges a client ip configuration, it can notify DNS with this clients ip-address and name. This is called **dynamic updates** or DDNS.

5.5.6. old reverse is forward in-addr.arpa

Reverse lookup is actually iomplemented as a forward lookup in the **in-addr.arpa** domain. This domain has 256 child domains (from 0.in-addr.arpa to 255.in-addr.arpa), with each child domain having again 256 child domains. And this twice more to a structure of over four billion (2 to the power 32) domains.

5.5.7. old ipv6

With rfc 3596 came ipv6 extensions for DNS. There is the AAAA record for ipv6 hosts on the network, and there is the **ip6.int** domain for reverse lookup (having 16 child domains from 0.ip6.int to f.ip6.int, each of those having again 16 child domains...and this 16 times.

5.5.8. old DNS security: file corruption

To mitigate file corruption on the **zone files** and the **bind configuration** files protect them with Unix permissions and take regular backups.

5.5.9. old DNS security: zone transfers

Limit zone transfers to certain ip addresses instead of to **any**. Nevermind that ip-addresses can be spoofed, still use this.

5.5.10. old DNS security: zone transfers, ip spoofing

You could setup DNSSEC (which is not the easiest to maintain) and with rfc 2845(tsig?) and with rfc 2930(tkey, but this is open to brute force), or you could disable all zone transfers and use a script with ssh to copy them manually.

5.5.11. old DNS security: queries

Allow recursion only from the local network, and iterative queries from outside only when necessary. This can be configured on master and slave servers.

```
view "internal" {
match-clients { 192.168.42/24; };
recursion yes;
...

};

view "external" {
match-clients { any; };
recursion no;
...

};
```

Or allow only queries from the local network.

```
options {
      allow-query { 192.168.42.0/24; localhost; };
};

zone "cobbaut.paul" {
      allow-query { any; };
};
```

Or only allow recursive queries from internal clients.

```
options {
        allow-recursion { 192.168.42.0/24; localhost; };
```

```
};
```

5.5.12. old DNS security: chrooted bind

Most Linux distributions allow an easy setup of bind in a **chrooted** environment.

5.5.13. old DNS security: DNSSEC

DNSSEC uses public/private keys to secure communications, this is described in rfc's 4033, 4034 and 4035.

5.5.14. old DNS security: root

Do not run bind as root. Do not run any application daemon as root.

Part IV. dhcp server

Table of Contents

Chapter 6. introduction to dhcp

Dynamic Host Configuration Protocol (or short **dhcp**) is a standard tcp/ip protocol that distributes ip configurations to clients. **dhcp** is defined in **rfc 2131** (before that it was defined as an update to **bootp** in rfc 1531/1541.

The alternative to **dhcp** is manually entering the ip configuration on each client computer.

6.1. four broadcasts

dhcp works with layer 2 broadcasts. A dhcp client that starts, will send a **dhcp discover** on the network. All **dhcp servers** (that have a lease available) will respond with a **dhcp offer**. The client will choose one of those offers and will send a **dhcp request** containing the chosen offer. The **dhcp server** usually responds with a **dhcp ack**(knowledge).

In wireshark it looks like this.

When this procedure is finished, then the client is allowed to use that ip-configuration until the end of its lease time.

6.2. picturing dhcp

Here we have a small network with two **dhcp servers** named DHCP-SRV1 and DHCP-SRV2 and two clients (SunWS1 and Mac42). All computers are connected by a hub or switch (pictured in the middle). All four computers have a cable to the hub (cables not pictured).

1. The client SunWS1 sends a **dhcp discover** on the network. All computers receive this broadcast.

2. Both **dhcp servers** answer with a **dhcp offer**. DHCP-SRV1 is a **dedicated dhcp server** and is faster in sending a **dhcp offer** than DHCP-SRV2 (who happens to also be a file server).

3. The client chooses the offer from DHCP-SRV1 and sends a **dhcp request** on the network.

4. DHCP-SRV1 answers with a **dhcp ack** (short for acknowledge).

All four broadcasts (or five when you count both offers) can be layer 2 ethernet broadcast to mac address **ff:ff:ff:ff:ff:ff** and a layer 3 ip broadcast to 255.255.255.255.

The same story can be read in **rfc 2131**.

6.3. installing a dhcp server

dhcp server for Debian/Mint

```
debian5:~# aptitude install dhcp3-server
Reading package lists... Done
Building dependency tree
Reading state information... Done
Reading extended state information
Initializing package states... Done
Reading task descriptions... Done
The following NEW packages will be installed:
  dhcp3-server
```

You get a configuration file with many examples.

```
debian5:~# ls -l /etc/dhcp3/dhcpd.conf
-rw-r--r-- 1 root root 3551 2011-04-10 21:23 /etc/dhcp3/dhcpd.conf
```

6.4. dhcp server for RHEL/CentOS

Installing is easy with **yum**.

```
[root@rhel71 ~]# yum install dhcp
Loaded plugins: product-id, subscription-manager
Resolving Dependencies
--> Running transaction check
---> Package dhcp.x86_64 12:4.2.5-36.el7 will be installed
--> Finished Dependency Resolution

Dependencies Resolved

================================================================================
 Package      Arch          Version            Repository              Size
================================================================================
Installing:
 dhcp         x86_64        12:4.2.5-36.el7    rhel-7-server-rpms      510 k

Transaction Summary
================================================================================
Install  1 Package

Total download size: 510 k
Installed size: 1.4 M
Is this ok [y/d/N]: y
Downloading packages:
dhcp-4.2.5-36.el7.x86_64.rpm                          | 510 kB   00:01
Running transaction check
Running transaction test
Transaction test succeeded
Running transaction
  Installing : 12:dhcp-4.2.5-36.el7.x86_64                               1/1
  Verifying  : 12:dhcp-4.2.5-36.el7.x86_64                               1/1

Installed:
  dhcp.x86_64 12:4.2.5-36.el7

Complete!
[root@rhel71 ~]#
```

After installing we get a **/etc/dhcp/dhcpd.conf** that points us to an example file named **dhcpd.conf.sample**.

```
[root@rhel71 ~]# cat /etc/dhcp/dhcpd.conf
#
# DHCP Server Configuration file.
#   see /usr/share/doc/dhcp*/dhcpd.conf.example
#   see dhcpd.conf(5) man page
#
[root@rhel71 ~]#
```

So we copy the sample and adjust it for our real situation. We name the copy **/etc/dhcp/dhcpd.conf**.

```
[root@rhel71 ~]# cp /usr/share/doc/dhcp-4.2.5/dhcpd.conf.example /etc/dhcp/dhcp\
d.conf
[root@rhel71 ~]# vi /etc/dhcp/dhcpd.conf
[root@rhel71 ~]# cat /etc/dhcp/dhcpd.conf
option domain-name "linux-training.be";
option domain-name-servers 10.42.42.42;
default-lease-time 600;
max-lease-time 7200;
log-facility local7;

subnet 10.42.0.0 netmask 255.255.0.0 {
  range 10.42.200.11 10.42.200.120;
  option routers 10.42.200.1;
}
[root@rhel71 ~]#
```

The 'routers' option is valid for the subnet alone, whereas the 'domain-name' option is global (for all subnets).

Time to start the server. Remember to use **systemctl start dhcpd** on RHEL7/CentOS7 and **service dhcpd start** on previous versions of RHEL/CentOS.

```
[root@rhel71 ~]# systemctl start dhcpd
[root@rhel71 ~]#
```

6.5. client reservations

You can reserve an ip configuration for a client using the mac address.

```
host pc42 {
hardware ethernet 11:22:33:44:55:66;
fixed-address 192.168.42.42;
}
```

You can add individual options to this reservation.

```
host pc42 {
hardware ethernet 11:22:33:44:55:66;
fixed-address 192.168.42.42;
option domain-name "linux-training.be";
option routers 192.168.42.1;
}
```

6.6. example config files

Below you see several sections of **/etc/dhcp/dhcpd.conf** on a **Debian 6** server.

```
# NetSec Antwerp Network
```

```
subnet 192.168.1.0 netmask 255.255.255.0 {
 range 192.168.1.20 192.168.1.199;
 option domain-name-servers ns1.netsec.local;
 option domain-name "netsec.local";
 option routers 192.168.1.1;
 option broadcast-address 192.168.1.255;
 default-lease-time 7200;
 max-lease-time 7200;
}
```

Above the general configuration for the network, with a pool of 180 addresses.

Below two client reservations:

```
#
# laptops
#

host mac {
   hardware ethernet 00:26:bb:xx:xx:xx;
   fixed-address mac.netsec.local;
}

host vmac {
   hardware ethernet 8c:7b:9d:xx:xx:xx;
   fixed-address vmac.netsec.local;
}
```

6.7. older example config files

For dhcpd.conf on Fedora with dynamic updates for a DNS domain.

```
[root@fedora14 ~]# cat /etc/dhcp/dhcpd.conf
authoritative;
include "/etc/rndc.key";

log-facility local6;

server-identifier    fedora14;
ddns-domainname  "office.linux-training.be";
ddns-update-style interim;
ddns-updates  on;
update-static-leases on;

option domain-name "office.linux-training.be";
option domain-name-servers 192.168.42.100;
option ip-forwarding off;

default-lease-time 1800;
max-lease-time  3600;

zone office.linux-training.be {
 primary 192.168.42.100;
}

subnet 192.168.4.0 netmask 255.255.255.0 {
 range 192.168.4.24 192.168.4.40;
}
```

Allowing any updates in the zone database (part of the named.conf configuration)

```
zone "office.linux-training.be" {
```

```
 type master;
 file "/var/named/db.office.linux-training.be";
 allow-transfer { any; };
 allow-update { any; };
};
```

Allowing secure key updates in the zone database (part of the named.conf configuration)

```
zone "office.linux-training.be" {
 type master;
 file "/var/named/db.office.linux-training.be";
 allow-transfer { any; };
 allow-update { key mykey; };
};
```

Sample key file contents:

```
[root@fedora14 ~]# cat /etc/rndc.key
key "rndc-key" {
 algorithm hmac-md5;
 secret "4Ykd58uIeUr3Ve6ad1qTfQ==";
};
```

Generate your own keys with **dnssec-keygen**.

How to include a key in a config file:

```
include "/etc/bind/rndc.key";
```

Also make sure that **bind** can write to your db.zone file (using chmod/chown). For Ubuntu this can be in /etc/bind, for Fedora in /var/named.

6.8. advanced dhcp

6.8.1. 80/20 rule

DHCP servers should not be a single point of failure. Let us discuss redundant dhcp server setups.

6.8.2. relay agent

To avoid having to place a dhcp server on every segment, we can use **dhcp relay agents**.

6.8.3. rogue dhcp servers

Rogue dhcp servers are a problem without a solution. For example accidental connection of a (believed to be simple) hub/switch to a network with an internal dhcp server.

6.8.4. dhcp and ddns

DHCP can dynamically update DNS when it configures a client computer. DDNS can be used with or without secure keys.

When set up properly records can be added automaticall to the zone file:

```
root@fedora14~# tail -2 /var/named/db.office.linux-training.be
ubu1010srv        A     192.168.42.151
                  TXT   "00dfbb15e144a273c3cf2d6ae933885782"
```

6.9. Practice: dhcp

1. Make sure you have a unique fixed ip address for your DNS and DHCP server (easier on the same machine).

2. Install DHCP and browse the explanation in the default configuration file /etc/dhcp/ dhcpd.conf or /etc/dhcp3/dhcpd.conf.

3. Decide on a valid scope and activate it.

4. Test with a client that your DHCP server works.

5. Use wireshark to capture the four broadcasts when a client receives an ip (for the first time).

6. Use wireshark to capture a DHCPNAK and a DHCPrelease.

7. Reserve a configuration for a particular client (using mac address).

8. Configure your DHCP/DNS server(s) with a proper hostname and domainname (/etc/ hosts, /etc/hostname, /etc/sysconfig/network on Fedora/RHEL, /etc/resolv.conf ...). You may need to disable NetworkManager on *buntu-desktops.

9. Make sure your DNS server still works, and is master over (at least) one domain.

There are several ways to do steps 10-11-12. Google is your friend in exploring DDNS with keys, with key-files or without keys.

10. Configure your DNS server to allow dynamic updates from your DHCP server.

11. Configure your DHCP server to send dynamic updates to your DNS server.

12. Test the working of Dynamic DNS.

Part V. iptables firewall

Table of Contents

Chapter 7. introduction to routers

What follows is a very brief introduction to using Linux as a router.

7.1. router or firewall

A **router** is a device that connects two networks. A **firewall** is a device that besides acting as a **router**, also contains (and implements) rules to determine whether packets are allowed to travel from one network to another. A firewall can be configured to block access based on networks, hosts, protocols and ports. Firewalls can also change the contents of packets while forwarding them.

7.2. packet forwarding

Packet forwarding means allowing packets to go from one network to another. When a multihomed host is connected to two different networks, and it allows packets to travel from one network to another through its two network interfaces, it is said to have enabled **packet forwarding**.

7.3. packet filtering

Packet filtering is very similar to packet forwarding, but every packet is individually tested against rules that decide on allowing or dropping the packet. The rules are stored by iptables.

7.4. stateful

A **stateful** firewall is an advancement over stateless firewalls that inspect every individual packet. A stateful firewall will keep a table of active connections, and is knowledgeable enough to recognise when new connections are part of an active session. Linux iptables is a stateful firewall.

7.5. nat (network address translation)

A **nat** device is a router that is also changing the source and/or target ip-address in packets. It is typically used to connect multiple computers in a private address range (rfc 1918) with the (public) internet. A **nat** can hide private addresses from the internet.

It is important to understand that people and vendors do not always use the right term when referring to a certain type of **nat**. Be sure you talk about the same thing. We can distuinguish several types of **nat**.

7.6. pat (port address translation)

nat often includes **pat**. A **pat** device is a router that is also changing the source and/or target tcp/udp port in packets. **pat** is Cisco terminology and is used by **snat**, **dnat**, **masquerading** and **port forwarding** in Linux. RFC 3022 calls it **NAPT** and defines the **nat/pat** combo as "traditional nat". A device sold to you as a nat-device will probably do **nat** and **pat**.

7.7. snat (source nat)

A **snat** device is changing the source ip-address when a packet passes our **nat**. **snat** configuration with iptables includes a fixed target source address.

7.8. masquerading

Masquerading is a form of **snat** that will hide the (private) source ip-addresses of your private network using a public ip-address. Masquerading is common on dynamic internet interfaces (broadband modem/routers). Masquerade configuration with iptables uses a dynamic target source address.

7.9. dnat (destination nat)

A **dnat** device is changing the destination ip-address when a packet passes our **nat**.

7.10. port forwarding

When static **dnat** is set up in a way that allows outside connections to enter our private network, then we call it **port forwarding**.

7.11. /proc/sys/net/ipv4/ip_forward

Whether a host is forwarding packets is defined in **/proc/sys/net/ipv4/ip_forward**. The following screenshot shows how to enable packet forwarding on Linux.

```
root@router~# echo 1 > /proc/sys/net/ipv4/ip_forward
```

The next command shows how to disable packet forwarding.

```
root@router~# echo 0 > /proc/sys/net/ipv4/ip_forward
```

Use cat to check if packet forwarding is enabled.

```
root@router~# cat /proc/sys/net/ipv4/ip_forward
```

7.12. /etc/sysctl.conf

By default, most Linux computers are not configured for automatic packet forwarding. To enable packet forwarding whenever the system starts, change the **net.ipv4.ip_forward** variable in **/etc/sysctl.conf** to the value 1.

```
root@router~# grep ip_forward /etc/sysctl.conf
net.ipv4.ip_forward = 0
```

7.13. sysctl

For more information, take a look at the man page of **sysctl**.

```
root@debian6~# man sysctl
root@debian6~# sysctl -a 2>/dev/null | grep ip_forward
net.ipv4.ip_forward = 0
```

7.14. practice: packet forwarding

0. You have the option to select (or create) an internal network when adding a network card in **VirtualBox** or **VMWare**. Use this option to create two internal networks. I named them **leftnet** and **rightnet**, but you can choose any other name.

> 🖧 **Network**
>
> Adapter 1: Intel PRO/1000 MT Desktop (Bridged Adapter, en1: AirPort)
> Adapter 2: Intel PRO/1000 MT Desktop (Internal Network, 'leftnet')
> Adapter 3: Intel PRO/1000 MT Desktop (Internal Network, 'rightnet')

1. Set up two Linux machines, one on **leftnet**, the other on **rightnet**. Make sure they both get an ip-address in the correct subnet. These two machines will be 'left' and 'right' from the 'router'.

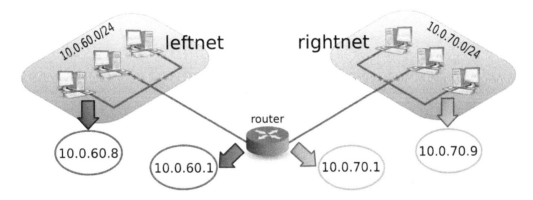

2. Set up a third Linux computer with three network cards, one on **leftnet**, the other on **rightnet**. This computer will be the 'router'. Complete the table below with the relevant names, ip-addresses and **mac-addresses**.

Table 7.1. Packet Forwarding Exercise

	leftnet computer	the router		rightnet computer
MAC				
IP				

3. How can you verify whether the **router** will allow packet forwarding by default or not ? Test that you can **ping** from the **router** to the two other machines, and from those two machines to the **router**. Use **arp -a** to make sure you are connected with the correct **mac addresses**.

4. **Ping** from the leftnet computer to the rightnet computer. Enable and/or disable packet forwarding on the **router** and verify what happens to the ping between the two networks. If you do not succeed in pinging between the two networks (on different subnets), then use a sniffer like **wireshark** or **tcpdump** to discover the problem.

5. Use **wireshark** or **tcpdump** -xx to answer the following questions. Does the source MAC change when a packet passes through the filter ? And the destination MAC ? What about source and destination IP-addresses ?

6. Remember the third network card on the router ? Connect this card to a LAN with internet connection. On many LAN's the command **dhclient eth0** just works (replace **eth0** with the correct interface).

```
root@router~# dhclient eth0
```

You now have a setup similar to this picture. What needs to be done to give internet access to **leftnet** and **rightnet**.

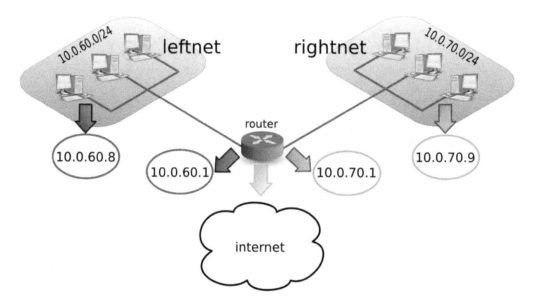

7.15. solution: packet forwarding

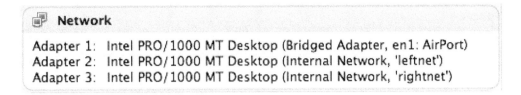

1. Set up two Linux machines, one on **leftnet**, the other on **rightnet**. Make sure they both get an ip-address in the correct subnet. These two machines will be 'left' and 'right' from the 'router'.

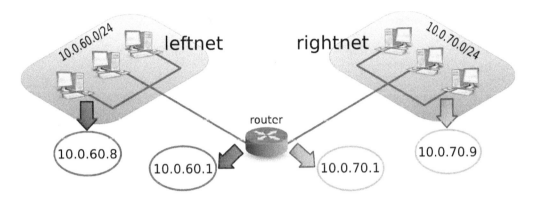

The ip configuration on your computers should be similar to the following two screenshots. Both machines must be in a different subnet (here 192.168.60.0/24 and 192.168.70.0/24). I created a little script on both machines to configure the interfaces.

```
root@left~# cat leftnet.sh
pkill dhclient
ifconfig eth0 192.168.60.8 netmask 255.255.255.0

root@right~# cat rightnet.sh
pkill dhclient
ifconfig eth0 192.168.70.9 netmask 255.255.255.0
```

2. Set up a third Linux computer with three network cards, one on **leftnet**, the other on **rightnet**. This computer will be the 'router'. Complete the table below with the relevant names, ip-addresses and mac-addresses.

```
root@router~# cat router.sh
ifconfig eth1 192.168.60.1 netmask 255.255.255.0
ifconfig eth2 192.168.70.1 netmask 255.255.255.0
#echo 1 > /proc/sys/net/ipv4/ip_forward
```

Your setup may use different ip and mac addresses than the ones in the table below.

Table 7.2. Packet Forwarding Solution

leftnet computer	the router		rightnet computer
08:00:27:f6:ab:b9	08:00:27:43:1f:5a	08:00:27:be:4a:6b	08:00:27:14:8b:17
192.168.60.8	192.168.60.1	192.168.70.1	192.168.70.9

3. How can you verify whether the **router** will allow packet forwarding by default or not ? Test that you can ping from the **router** to the two other machines, and from those two machines to the **router**. Use **arp -a** to make sure you are connected with the correct **mac addresses**.

This can be done with "**grep ip_forward /etc/sysctl.conf**" (1 is enabled, 0 is disabled) or with **sysctl -a | grep ip_for**.

```
root@router~# grep ip_for /etc/sysctl.conf
net.ipv4.ip_forward = 0
```

4. Ping from the leftnet computer to the rightnet computer. Enable and/or disable packet forwarding on the **router** and verify what happens to the ping between the two networks. If you do not succeed in pinging between the two networks (on different subnets), then use a sniffer like wireshark or tcpdump to discover the problem.

Did you forget to add a **default gateway** to the LAN machines ? Use **route add default gw 'ip-address'**.

```
root@left~# route add default gw 192.168.60.1
```

```
root@right~# route add default gw 192.168.70.1
```

You should be able to ping when packet forwarding is enabled (and both default gateways are properly configured). The ping will not work when packet forwarding is disabled or when gateways are not configured correctly.

5. Use wireshark or tcpdump -xx to answer the following questions. Does the source MAC change when a packet passes through the filter ? And the destination MAC ? What about source and destination IP-addresses ?

Both MAC addresses are changed when passing the router. Use **tcpdump -xx** like this:

```
root@router~# tcpdump -xx -i eth1
```

```
root@router~# tcpdump -xx -i eth2
```

6. Remember the third network card on the router ? Connect this card to a LAN with internet connection. On many LAN's the command **dhclient eth0** just works (replace **eth0** with the correct interface.

```
root@router~# dhclient eth0
```

You now have a setup similar to this picture. What needs to be done to give internet access to **leftnet** and **rightnet**.

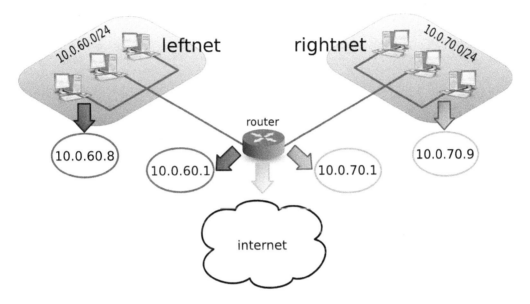

The clients on **leftnet** and **rightnet** need a working **dns server**. We use one of Google's dns servers here.

```
echo nameserver 8.8.8.8 > /etc/resolv.conf
```

Chapter 8. iptables firewall

This chapter introduces some simple firewall rules and how to configure them with **iptables**.

iptables is an application that allows a user to configure the firewall functionality built into the **Linux** kernel.

8.1. iptables tables

By default there are three **tables** in the kernel that contain sets of rules.

The **filter table** is used for packet filtering.

```
root@debian6~# iptables -t filter -L
Chain INPUT (policy ACCEPT)
target     prot opt source               destination

Chain FORWARD (policy ACCEPT)
target     prot opt source               destination

Chain OUTPUT (policy ACCEPT)
target     prot opt source               destination
```

The **nat table** is used for address translation.

```
root@debian6~# iptables -t nat -L
Chain PREROUTING (policy ACCEPT)
target     prot opt source               destination

Chain POSTROUTING (policy ACCEPT)
target     prot opt source               destination

Chain OUTPUT (policy ACCEPT)
target     prot opt source               destination
```

The **mangle table** can be used for special-purpose processing of packets.

Series of rules in each table are called a **chain**. We will discuss chains and the nat table later in this chapter.

8.2. starting and stopping iptables

The following screenshot shows how to stop and start **iptables** on Red Hat/Fedora/CentOS and compatible distributions.

```
[root@centos6 ~]# service iptables stop
[root@centos6 ~]# service iptables start
iptables: Applying firewall rules                              [ ok ]
[root@centos6 ~]#
```

Debian and *buntu distributions do not have this script, but allow for an uninstall.

```
root@debian6~# aptitude purge iptables
```

8.3. the filter table

8.3.1. about packet filtering

Packet filtering is a bit more than **packet forwarding**. While **packet forwarding** uses only a routing table to make decisions, **packet filtering** also uses a list of rules. The kernel will inspect packets and decide based on these rules what to do with each packet.

8.3.2. filter table

The filter table in **iptables** has three chains (sets of rules). The INPUT chain is used for any packet coming into the system. The OUTPUT chain is for any packet leaving the system. And the FORWARD chain is for packets that are forwarded (routed) through the system.

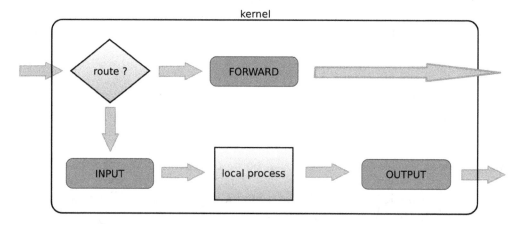

The screenshot below shows how to list the filter table and all its rules.

```
[root@RHEL5 ~]# iptables -t filter -nL
Chain INPUT (policy ACCEPT)
target     prot opt source               destination

Chain FORWARD (policy ACCEPT)
target     prot opt source               destination

Chain OUTPUT (policy ACCEPT)
target     prot opt source               destination
[root@RHEL5 ~]#
```

As you can see, all three chains in the filter table are set to ACCEPT everything. ACCEPT is the default behaviour.

8.3.3. setting default rules

The default for the default rule is indeed to ACCEPT everything. This is not the most secure firewall.

A more secure setup would be to DROP everything. A package that is **dropped** will not continue in any chain, and no warning or error will be sent anywhere.

The below commands lock down a computer. Do not execute these commands inside a remote ssh shell.

```
root@debianpaul~# iptables -P INPUT DROP
root@debianpaul~# iptables -P OUTPUT DROP
root@debianpaul~# iptables -P FORWARD DROP
root@debianpaul~# iptables -L
Chain INPUT (policy DROP)
target     prot opt source              destination

Chain FORWARD (policy DROP)
target     prot opt source              destination

Chain OUTPUT (policy DROP)
target     prot opt source              destination
```

8.3.4. changing policy rules

To start, let's set the default policy for all three chains to drop everything. Note that you might lose your connection when typing this over ssh ;-).

```
[root@RHEL5 ~]# iptables -P INPUT DROP
[root@RHEL5 ~]# iptables -P FORWARD DROP
[root@RHEL5 ~]# iptables -P OUTPUT DROP
```

Next, we allow the server to use its own loopback device (this allows the server to access its services running on localhost). We first append a rule to the INPUT chain to allow (ACCEPT) traffic from the lo (loopback) interface, then we do the same to allow packets to leave the system through the loopback interface.

```
[root@RHEL5 ~]# iptables -A INPUT -i lo -j ACCEPT
[root@RHEL5 ~]# iptables -A OUTPUT -o lo -j ACCEPT
```

Looking at the filter table again (omitting -t filter because it is the default table).

```
[root@RHEL5 ~]# iptables -nL
Chain INPUT (policy DROP)
target     prot opt source              destination
ACCEPT     all  --  0.0.0.0/0           0.0.0.0/0

Chain FORWARD (policy DROP)
target     prot opt source              destination

Chain OUTPUT (policy DROP)
target     prot opt source              destination
ACCEPT     all  --  0.0.0.0/0           0.0.0.0/0
```

8.3.5. Allowing ssh over eth0

This example show how to add two rules to allow ssh access to your system from outside.

```
[root@RHEL5 ~]# iptables -A INPUT -i eth0 -p tcp --dport 22 -j ACCEPT
[root@RHEL5 ~]# iptables -A OUTPUT -o eth0 -p tcp --sport 22 -j ACCEPT
```

The filter table will look something like this screenshot (note that -v is added for more verbose output).

```
[root@RHEL5 ~]# iptables -nvL
Chain INPUT (policy DROP 7 packets, 609 bytes)
 pkts bytes target prot opt in     out   source      destination
    0     0 ACCEPT all  --  lo     *     0.0.0.0/0   0.0.0.0/0
    0     0 ACCEPT tcp  --  eth0   *     0.0.0.0/0   0.0.0.0/0  tcp dpt:22

Chain FORWARD (policy DROP 0 packets, 0 bytes)
 pkts bytes target prot opt in     out   source      destination

Chain OUTPUT (policy DROP 3 packets, 228 bytes)
 pkts bytes target prot opt in     out   source      destination
    0     0 ACCEPT all  --  *      lo    0.0.0.0/0   0.0.0.0/0
    0     0 ACCEPT tcp  --  *      eth0  0.0.0.0/0   0.0.0.0/0  tcp spt:22
[root@RHEL5 ~]#
```

8.3.6. Allowing access from a subnet

This example shows how to allow access from any computer in the 10.1.1.0/24 network, but only through eth1. There is no port (application) limitation here.

```
[root@RHEL5 ~]# iptables -A INPUT -i eth1 -s 10.1.1.0/24 -p tcp -j ACCEPT
[root@RHEL5 ~]# iptables -A OUTPUT -o eth1 -d 10.1.1.0/24 -p tcp -j ACCEPT
```

Together with the previous examples, the policy is expanding.

```
[root@RHEL5 ~]# iptables -nvL
Chain INPUT (policy DROP 7 packets, 609 bytes)
 pkts bytes target prot opt in     out   source       destination
    0     0 ACCEPT all  --  lo     *     0.0.0.0/0    0.0.0.0/0
    0     0 ACCEPT tcp  --  eth0   *     0.0.0.0/0    0.0.0.0/0  tcp dpt:22
    0     0 ACCEPT tcp  --  eth1   *     10.1.1.0/24  0.0.0.0/0

Chain FORWARD (policy DROP 0 packets, 0 bytes)
 pkts bytes target prot opt in     out   source       destination

Chain OUTPUT (policy DROP 3 packets, 228 bytes)
 pkts bytes target prot opt in     out   source       destination
    0     0 ACCEPT all  --  *      lo    0.0.0.0/0    0.0.0.0/0
    0     0 ACCEPT tcp  --  *      eth0  0.0.0.0/0    0.0.0.0/0  tcp spt:22
    0     0 ACCEPT tcp  --  *      eth1  0.0.0.0/0    10.1.1.0/24
```

8.3.7. iptables save

Use **iptables save** to automatically implement these rules when the firewall is (re)started.

```
[root@RHEL5 ~]# /etc/init.d/iptables save
Saving firewall rules to /etc/sysconfig/iptables:          [  OK  ]
[root@RHEL5 ~]#
```

8.3.8. scripting example

You can write a simple script for these rules. Below is an example script that implements the firewall rules that you saw before in this chapter.

```
#!/bin/bash
# first cleanup everything
iptables -t filter -F
iptables -t filter -X
iptables -t nat -F
iptables -t nat -X

# default drop
iptables -P INPUT DROP
iptables -P FORWARD DROP
iptables -P OUTPUT DROP

# allow loopback device
iptables -A INPUT -i lo -j ACCEPT
iptables -A OUTPUT -o lo -j ACCEPT

# allow ssh over eth0 from outside to system
iptables -A INPUT -i eth0 -p tcp --dport 22 -j ACCEPT
iptables -A OUTPUT -o eth0 -p tcp --sport 22 -j ACCEPT

# allow any traffic from 10.1.1.0/24 to system
iptables -A INPUT -i eth1 -s 10.1.1.0/24 -p tcp -j ACCEPT
iptables -A OUTPUT -o eth1 -d 10.1.1.0/24 -p tcp -j ACCEPT
```

8.3.9. Allowing ICMP(ping)

When you enable iptables, you will get an **'Operation not permitted'** message when trying to ping other hosts.

```
[root@RHEL5 ~# ping 192.168.187.130
PING 192.168.187.130 (192.168.187.130) 56(84) bytes of data.
ping: sendmsg: Operation not permitted
ping: sendmsg: Operation not permitted
```

The screenshot below shows you how to setup iptables to allow a ping from or to your machine.

```
[root@RHEL5 ~]# iptables -A INPUT -p icmp --icmp-type any -j ACCEPT
[root@RHEL5 ~]# iptables -A OUTPUT -p icmp --icmp-type any -j ACCEPT
```

The previous two lines do not allow other computers to route ping messages through your router, because it only handles INPUT and OUTPUT. For routing of ping, you will need to enable it on the FORWARD chain. The following command enables routing of icmp messages between networks.

```
[root@RHEL5 ~]# iptables -A FORWARD -p icmp --icmp-type any -j ACCEPT
```

8.4. practice: packet filtering

1. Make sure you can ssh to your router-system when iptables is active.

2. Make sure you can ping to your router-system when iptables is active.

3. Define one of your networks as 'internal' and the other as 'external'. Configure the router to allow visits to a website (http) to go from the internal network to the external network (but not in the other direction).

4. Make sure the internal network can ssh to the external, but not the other way around.

8.5. solution: packet filtering

A possible solution, where leftnet is the internal and rightnet is the external network.

```
#!/bin/bash

# first cleanup everything
iptables -t filter -F
iptables -t filter -X
iptables -t nat -F
iptables -t nat -X

# default drop
iptables -P INPUT DROP
iptables -P FORWARD DROP
iptables -P OUTPUT DROP

# allow loopback device
iptables -A INPUT -i lo -j ACCEPT
iptables -A OUTPUT -o lo -j ACCEPT

# question 1: allow ssh over eth0
iptables -A INPUT -i eth0 -p tcp --dport 22 -j ACCEPT
iptables -A OUTPUT -o eth0 -p tcp --sport 22 -j ACCEPT

# question 2: Allow icmp(ping) anywhere
iptables -A INPUT -p icmp --icmp-type any -j ACCEPT
iptables -A FORWARD -p icmp --icmp-type any -j ACCEPT
iptables -A OUTPUT -p icmp --icmp-type any -j ACCEPT

# question 3: allow http from internal(leftnet) to external(rightnet)
iptables -A FORWARD -i eth1 -o eth2 -p tcp --dport 80 -j ACCEPT
iptables -A FORWARD -i eth2 -o eth1 -p tcp --sport 80 -j ACCEPT

# question 4: allow ssh from internal(leftnet) to external(rightnet)
iptables -A FORWARD -i eth1 -o eth2 -p tcp --dport 22 -j ACCEPT
iptables -A FORWARD -i eth2 -o eth1 -p tcp --sport 22 -j ACCEPT

# allow http from external(rightnet) to internal(leftnet)
# iptables -A FORWARD -i eth2 -o eth1 -p tcp --dport 80 -j ACCEPT
# iptables -A FORWARD -i eth1 -o eth2 -p tcp --sport 80 -j ACCEPT

# allow rpcinfo over eth0 from outside to system
# iptables -A INPUT -i eth2 -p tcp --dport 111 -j ACCEPT
# iptables -A OUTPUT -o eth2 -p tcp --sport 111 -j ACCEPT
```

8.6. network address translation

8.6.1. about NAT

A NAT device is a router that is also changing the source and/or target ip-address in packets. It is typically used to connect multiple computers in a private address range with the (public) internet. A NAT can hide private addresses from the internet.

NAT was developed to mitigate the use of real ip addresses, to allow private address ranges to reach the internet and back, and to not disclose details about internal networks to the outside.

The nat table in iptables adds two new chains. PREROUTING allows altering of packets before they reach the INPUT chain. POSTROUTING allows altering packets after they exit the OUTPUT chain.

Use **iptables -t nat -nvL** to look at the NAT table. The screenshot below shows an empty NAT table.

```
[root@RHEL5 ~]# iptables -t nat -nL
Chain PREROUTING (policy ACCEPT)
target     prot opt source               destination

Chain POSTROUTING (policy ACCEPT)
target     prot opt source               destination

Chain OUTPUT (policy ACCEPT)
target     prot opt source               destination
[root@RHEL5 ~]#
```

8.6.2. SNAT (Source NAT)

The goal of source nat is to change the source address inside a packet before it leaves the system (e.g. to the internet). The destination will return the packet to the NAT-device. This means our NAT-device will need to keep a table in memory of all the packets it changed, so it can deliver the packet to the original source (e.g. in the private network).

Because SNAT is about packets leaving the system, it uses the POSTROUTING chain.

Here is an example SNAT rule. The rule says that packets coming from 10.1.1.0/24 network and exiting via eth1 will get the source ip-address set to 11.12.13.14. (Note that this is a one line command!)

```
iptables -t nat -A POSTROUTING -o eth1 -s 10.1.1.0/24 -j SNAT \
--to-source 11.12.13.14
```

Of course there must exist a proper iptables filter setup to allow the packet to traverse from one network to the other.

8.6.3. SNAT example setup

This example script uses a typical nat setup. The internal (eth0) network has access via SNAT to external (eth1) webservers (port 80).

```
#!/bin/bash
#
# iptables script for simple classic nat websurfing
# eth0 is internal network, eth1 is internet
#
echo 0 > /proc/sys/net/ipv4/ip_forward
iptables -P INPUT ACCEPT
iptables -P OUTPUT ACCEPT
iptables -P FORWARD DROP
iptables -A FORWARD -i eth0 -o eth1 -s 10.1.1.0/24 -p tcp \
--dport 80 -j ACCEPT
iptables -A FORWARD -i eth1 -o eth0 -d 10.1.1.0/24 -p tcp \
--sport 80 -j ACCEPT
iptables -t nat -A POSTROUTING -o eth1 -s 10.1.1.0/24 -j SNAT \
--to-source 11.12.13.14
echo 1 > /proc/sys/net/ipv4/ip_forward
```

8.6.4. IP masquerading

IP masquerading is very similar to SNAT, but is meant for dynamic interfaces. Typical example are broadband 'router/modems' connected to the internet and receiving a different ip-address from the isp, each time they are cold-booted.

The only change needed to convert the SNAT script to a masquerading is one line.

```
iptables -t nat -A POSTROUTING -o eth1 -s 10.1.1.0/24 -j MASQUERADE
```

8.6.5. DNAT (Destination NAT)

DNAT is typically used to allow packets from the internet to be redirected to an internal server (in your DMZ) and in a private address range that is inaccessible directly form the internet.

This example script allows internet users to reach your internal (192.168.1.99) server via ssh (port 22).

```
#!/bin/bash
#
# iptables script for DNAT
# eth0 is internal network, eth1 is internet
#
echo 0 > /proc/sys/net/ipv4/ip_forward
iptables -P INPUT ACCEPT
iptables -P OUTPUT ACCEPT
iptables -P FORWARD DROP
iptables -A FORWARD -i eth0 -o eth1 -s 10.1.1.0/24 -j ACCEPT
iptables -A FORWARD -i eth1 -o eth0 -p tcp --dport 22 -j ACCEPT
iptables -t nat -A PREROUTING -i eth1 -p tcp --dport 22 \
-j DNAT --to-destination 10.1.1.99
echo 1 > /proc/sys/net/ipv4/ip_forward
```

Part VI. Introduction to Samba

Table of Contents

Chapter 9. introduction to samba

This introduction to the Samba server simply explains how to install Samba 3 and briefly mentions the SMB protocol.

9.1. verify installed version

9.1.1. .rpm based distributions

To see the version of samba installed on Red Hat, Fedora or CentOS use **rpm -q samba**.

```
[root@RHEL52 ~]# rpm -q samba
samba-3.0.28-1.el5_2.1
```

The screenshot above shows that RHEL5 has **Samba** version 3.0 installed. The last number in the Samba version counts the number of updates or patches.

Below the same command on a more recent version of CentOS with Samba version 3.5 installed.

```
[root@centos6 ~]# rpm -q samba
samba-3.5.10-116.el6_2.i686
```

9.1.2. .deb based distributions

Use **dpkg -l** or **aptitide show** on Debian or Ubuntu. Both Debian 7.0 (Wheezy) and Ubuntu 12.04 (Precise) use version 3.6.3 of the Samba server.

```
root@debian7~# aptitude show samba | grep Version
Version: 2:3.6.3-1
```

Ubuntu 12.04 is currently at Samba version 3.6.3.

```
root@ubu1204:~# dpkg -l samba | tail -1
ii samba 2:3.6.3-2ubuntu2.1 SMB/CIFS file, print, and login server for Unix
```

9.2. installing samba

9.2.1. .rpm based distributions

Samba is installed by default on Red Hat Enterprise Linux. If Samba is not yet installed, then you can use the graphical menu (Applications -- System Settings -- Add/Remove Applications) and select "Windows File Server" in the Server section. The non-graphical way is to use **rpm** or **yum**.

When you downloaded the .rpm file, you can install Samba like this.

```
[paul@RHEL52 ~]$ rpm -i samba-3.0.28-1.el5_2.1.rpm
```

When you have a subscription to RHN (Red Hat Network), then **yum** is an easy tool to use. This **yum** command works by default on Fedora and CentOS.

```
[root@centos6 ~]# yum install samba
```

9.2.2. .deb based distributions

Ubuntu and Debian users can use the **aptitude** program (or use a graphical tool like Synaptic).

```
root@debian7~# aptitude install samba
The following NEW packages will be installed:
  samba samba-common{a} samba-common-bin{a} tdb-tools{a}
0 packages upgraded, 4 newly installed, 0 to remove and 1 not upgraded.
Need to get 15.1 MB of archives. After unpacking 42.9 MB will be used.
Do you want to continue? [Y/n/?]
...
```

9.3. documentation

9.3.1. samba howto

Samba comes with excellent documentation in html and pdf format (and also as a free download from samba.org and it is for sale as a printed book).

The documentation is a separate package, so install it if you want it on the server itself.

```
[root@centos6 ~]# yum install samba-doc
...
[root@centos6 ~]# ls -l /usr/share/doc/samba-doc-3.5.10/
total 10916
drwxr-xr-x. 6 root root    4096 May  6 15:50 htmldocs
-rw-r--r--. 1 root root 4605496 Jun 14  2011 Samba3-ByExample.pdf
-rw-r--r--. 1 root root  608260 Jun 14  2011 Samba3-Developers-Guide.pdf
-rw-r--r--. 1 root root 5954602 Jun 14  2011 Samba3-HOWTO.pdf
```

This action is very similar on Ubuntu and Debian except that the pdf files are in a separate package named **samba-doc-pdf**.

```
root@ubu1204:~# aptitude install samba-doc-pdf
The following NEW packages will be installed:
  samba-doc-pdf
...
```

9.3.2. samba by example

Besides the howto, there is also an excellent book called **Samba By Example** (again available as printed edition in shops, and as a free pdf and html).

9.4. starting and stopping samba

You can start the daemons by invoking **/etc/init.d/smb start** (some systems use **/etc/init.d/samba**) on any linux.

```
root@laika:~# /etc/init.d/samba stop
 * Stopping Samba daemons                                  [ OK ]
root@laika:~# /etc/init.d/samba start
 * Starting Samba daemons                                  [ OK ]
root@laika:~# /etc/init.d/samba restart
 * Stopping Samba daemons                                  [ OK ]
 * Starting Samba daemons                                  [ OK ]
root@laika:~# /etc/init.d/samba status
 * SMBD is running                                         [ OK ]
```

Red Hat derived systems are happy with **service smb start**.

```
[root@RHEL4b ~]# /etc/init.d/smb start
Starting SMB services:                              [  OK  ]
Starting NMB services:                              [  OK  ]
[root@RHEL4b ~]# service smb restart
Shutting down SMB services:                         [  OK  ]
Shutting down NMB services:                         [  OK  ]
Starting SMB services:                              [  OK  ]
Starting NMB services:                              [  OK  ]
[root@RHEL4b ~]#
```

9.5. samba daemons

Samba 3 consists of three daemons, they are named **nmbd**, **smbd** and **winbindd**.

9.5.1. nmbd

The **nmbd** daemon takes care of all the names and naming. It registers and resolves names, and handles browsing. According to the Samba documentation, it should be the first daemon to start.

```
[root@RHEL52 ~]# ps -C nmbd
  PID TTY          TIME CMD
 5681 ?        00:00:00 nmbd
```

9.5.2. smbd

The **smbd** daemon manages file transfers and authentication.

```
[root@RHEL52 ~]# ps -C smbd
  PID TTY          TIME CMD
 5678 ?        00:00:00 smbd
 5683 ?        00:00:00 smbd
```

9.5.3. winbindd

The **winbind daemon** (winbindd) is only started to handle Microsoft Windows domain membership.

Note that **winbindd** is started by the **/etc/init.d/winbind** script (two dd's for the daemon and only one d for the script).

```
[root@RHEL52 ~]# /etc/init.d/winbind start
Starting Winbind services:                          [  OK  ]
[root@RHEL52 ~]# ps -C winbindd
  PID TTY          TIME CMD
 5752 ?        00:00:00 winbindd
 5754 ?        00:00:00 winbindd
```

On Debian and Ubuntu, the winbindd daemon is installed via a separate package called **winbind**.

9.6. the SMB protocol

9.6.1. brief history

Development of this protocol was started by **IBM** in the early eighties. By the end of the eighties, most develpment was done by **Microsoft**. SMB is an application level protocol designed to run on top of NetBIOS/NetBEUI, but can also be run on top of tcp/ip.

In 1996 Microsoft was asked to document the protocol. They submitted CIFS (Common Internet File System) as an internet draft, but it never got final rfc status.

In 2004 the European Union decided Microsoft should document the protocol to enable other developers to write compatible software. December 20th 2007 Microsoft came to an agreement. The Samba team now has access to SMB/CIFS, Windows for Workgroups and Active Directory documentation.

9.6.2. broadcasting protocol

SMB uses the NetBIOS **service location protocol**, which is a broadcasting protocol. This means that NetBIOS names have to be unique on the network (even when you have different IP-addresses). Having duplicate names on an SMB network can seriously harm communications.

9.6.3. NetBIOS names

NetBIOS names are similar to **hostnames**, but are always uppercase and only 15 characters in length. Microsoft Windows computers and Samba servers will broadcast this name on the network.

9.6.4. network bandwidth

Having many broadcasting SMB/CIFS computers on your network can cause bandwidth issues. A solution can be the use of a **NetBIOS name server** (NBNS) like **WINS** (Windows Internet Naming Service).

9.7. practice: introduction to samba

0. !! Make sure you know your student number, anything *ANYTHING* you name must include your student number!

1. Verify that you can logon to a Linux/Unix computer. Write down the name and ip address of this computer.

2. Do the same for all the other (virtual) machines available to you.

3. Verify networking by pinging the computer, edit the appropriate hosts files so you can use names. Test the names by pinging them.

4. Make sure Samba is installed, write down the version of Samba.

5. Open the Official Samba-3 howto pdf file that is installed on your computer. How many A4 pages is this file ? Then look at the same pdf on samba.org, it is updated regularly.

6. Stop the Samba server.

Chapter 10. getting started with samba

10.1. /etc/samba/smb.conf

10.1.1. smbd -b

Samba configuration is done in the **smb.conf** file. The file can be edited manually, or you can use a web based interface like webmin or swat to manage it. The file is usually located in /etc/samba. You can find the exact location with **smbd -b**.

```
[root@RHEL4b ~]# smbd -b | grep CONFIGFILE
CONFIGFILE: /etc/samba/smb.conf
```

10.1.2. the default smb.conf

The default smb.conf file contains a lot of examples with explanations.

```
[paul@RHEL4b ~]$ ls -l /etc/samba/smb.conf
-rw-r--r--  1 root root 10836 May 30 23:08 /etc/samba/smb.conf
```

Also on Ubuntu and Debian, smb.conf is packed with samples and explanations.

```
paul@laika:~$ ls -l /etc/samba/smb.conf
-rw-r--r-- 1 root root 10515 2007-05-24 00:21 /etc/samba/smb.conf
```

10.1.3. minimal smb.conf

Below is an example of a very minimalistic **smb.conf**. It allows samba to start, and to be visible to other computers (Microsoft shows computers in Network Neighborhood or My Network Places).

```
[paul@RHEL4b ~]$ cat /etc/samba/smb.conf
[global]
workgroup = WORKGROUP
[firstshare]
path = /srv/samba/public
```

10.1.4. net view

Below is a screenshot of the **net view** command on Microsoft Windows Server 2003 sp2. It shows how a Red Hat Enterprise Linux 5.3 and a Ubuntu 9.04 Samba server, both with a minimalistic smb.conf, are visible to Microsoft computers nearby.

```
C:\Documents and Settings\Administrator>net view
Server Name            Remark
-------------------------------------------------------------------------
\\LAIKA                Samba 3.3.2
\\RHEL53               Samba 3.0.33-3.7.el5
\\W2003
The command completed successfully.
```

10.1.5. long lines in smb.conf

Some parameters in smb.conf can get a long list of values behind them. You can continue a line (for clarity) on the next by ending the line with a backslash.

```
valid users = Serena, Venus, Lindsay \
```

```
                Kim, Justine, Sabine \
                Amelie, Marie, Suzanne
```

10.1.6. curious smb.conf

Curious but true: smb.conf accepts synonyms like **create mode** and **create mask**, and (sometimes) minor spelling errors like **browsable** and **browseable**. And on occasion you can even switch words, the **guest only** parameter is identical to **only guest**. And **writable = yes** is the same as **readonly = no**.

10.1.7. man smb.conf

You can access a lot of documentation when typing **man smb.conf**.

```
[root@RHEL4b samba]# apropos samba
cupsaddsmb       (8)   - export printers to samba for windows clients
lmhosts          (5)   - The Samba NetBIOS hosts file
net              (8)   - Tool for administration of Samba and remote CIFS servers
pdbedit          (8)   - manage the SAM database (Database of Samba Users)
samba            (7)   - A Windows SMB/CIFS fileserver for UNIX
smb.conf [smb]   (5)   - The configuration file for the Samba suite
smbpasswd        (5)   - The Samba encrypted password file
smbstatus        (1)   - report on current Samba connections
swat             (8)   - Samba Web Administration Tool
tdbbackup        (8)   - tool for backing up and ... of samba .tdb files
[root@RHEL4b samba]#
```

10.2. /usr/bin/testparm

10.2.1. syntax check smb.conf

To verify the syntax of the smb.conf file, you can use **testparm**.

```
[paul@RHEL4b ~]$ testparm
Load smb config files from /etc/samba/smb.conf
Processing section "[firstshare]"
Loaded services file OK.
Server role: ROLE_STANDALONE
Press enter to see a dump of your service definitions
```

10.2.2. testparm -v

An interesting option is **testparm -v**, which will output all the global options with their default value.

```
[root@RHEL52 ~]# testparm -v | head
Load smb config files from /etc/samba/smb.conf
Processing section "[pub0]"
Processing section "[global$]"
Loaded services file OK.
Server role: ROLE_STANDALONE
Press enter to see a dump of your service definitions

[global]
 dos charset = CP850
 unix charset = UTF-8
 display charset = LOCALE
 workgroup = WORKGROUP
```

```
realm =
netbios name = TEACHER0
netbios aliases =
netbios scope =
server string = Samba 3.0.28-1.el5_2.1
...
```

There were about 350 default values for smb.conf parameters in Samba 3.0.x. This number grew to almost 400 in Samba 3.5.x.

10.2.3. testparm -s

The samba daemons are constantly (once every 60 seconds) checking the smb.conf file, so it is good practice to keep this file small. But it is also good practice to document your samba configuration, and to explicitly set options that have the same default values. The **testparm -s** option allows you to do both. It will output the smallest possible samba configuration file, while retaining all your settings. The idea is to have your samba configuration in another file (like smb.conf.full) and let testparm parse this for you. The screenshot below shows you how. First the smb.conf.full file with the explicitly set option workgroup to WORKGROUP.

```
[root@RHEL4b samba]# cat smb.conf.full
[global]
workgroup = WORKGROUP

# This is a demo of a documented smb.conf
# These two lines are removed by testparm -s

server string = Public Test Server

[firstshare]
path = /srv/samba/public
```

Next, we execute testparm with the -s option, and redirect stdout to the real **smb.conf** file.

```
[root@RHEL4b samba]# testparm -s smb.conf.full > smb.conf
Load smb config files from smb.conf.full
Processing section "[firstshare]"
Loaded services file OK.
```

And below is the end result. The two comment lines and the default option are no longer there.

```
[root@RHEL4b samba]# cat smb.conf
# Global parameters
[global]
server string = Public Test Server

[firstshare]
path = /srv/samba/public
[root@RHEL4b samba]#
```

10.3. /usr/bin/smbclient

10.3.1. smbclient looking at Samba

With **smbclient** you can see browsing and share information from your smb server. It will display all your shares, your workgroup, and the name of the Master Browser. The -N switch is added to avoid having to enter an empty password. The -L switch is followed by the name of the host to check.

```
[root@RHEL4b init.d]# smbclient -NL rhel4b
Anonymous login successful
Domain=[WORKGROUP] OS=[Unix] Server=[Samba 3.0.10-1.4E.9]

Sharename      Type        Comment
---------      ----        -------
firstshare     Disk
IPC$           IPC         IPC Service (Public Test Server)
ADMIN$         IPC         IPC Service (Public Test Server)
Anonymous login successful
Domain=[WORKGROUP] OS=[Unix] Server=[Samba 3.0.10-1.4E.9]

Server               Comment
---------            -------
RHEL4B               Public Test Server
WINXP

Workgroup            Master
---------            -------
WORKGROUP            WINXP
```

10.3.2. smbclient anonymous

The screenshot below uses **smbclient** to display information about a remote smb server (in this case a computer with Ubuntu 11.10).

```
root@ubu1110:/etc/samba# testparm smbclient -NL 127.0.0.1
Anonymous login successful
Domain=[LINUXTR] OS=[Unix] Server=[Samba 3.5.11]
    Sharename      Type        Comment
    ---------      ----        -------
    share1         Disk
    IPC$           IPC         IPC Service (Samba 3.5.11)
Anonymous login successful
Domain=[LINUXTR] OS=[Unix] Server=[Samba 3.5.11]
    Server               Comment
    ---------            -------

    Workgroup            Master
    ---------            -------
    LINUXTR              DEBIAN6
    WORKGROUP            UBU1110
```

10.3.3. smbclient with credentials

Windows versions after xp sp2 and 2003 sp1 do not accept guest access (the NT_STATUS_ACCESS_DENIED error). This example shows how to provide credentials with **smbclient**.

```
[paul@RHEL53 ~]$ smbclient -L w2003 -U administrator%stargate
Domain=[W2003] OS=[Windows Server 2003 3790 Service Pack 2] Server=...

    Sharename      Type        Comment
    ---------      ----        -------
    C$             Disk        Default share
```

```
IPC$            IPC       Remote IPC
ADMIN$          Disk      Remote Admin
...
```

10.4. /usr/bin/smbtree

Another useful tool to troubleshoot Samba or simply to browse the SMB network is **smbtree**. In its simplest form, smbtree will do an anonymous browsing on the local subnet. displaying all SMB computers and (if authorized) their shares.

Let's take a look at two screenshots of smbtree in action (with blank password). The first one is taken immediately after booting four different computers (one MS Windows 2000, one MS Windows xp, one MS Windows 2003 and one RHEL 4 with Samba 3.0.10).

```
[paul@RHEL4b ~]$ smbtree
Password:
WORKGROUP
PEGASUS
 \\WINXP
 \\RHEL4B                           Pegasus Domain Member Server
Error connecting to 127.0.0.1 (Connection refused)
cli_full_connection: failed to connect to RHEL4B<20> (127.0.0.1)
 \\HM2003
[paul@RHEL4b ~]$
```

The information displayed in the previous screenshot looks incomplete. The browsing elections are still ongoing, the browse list is not yet distributed to all clients by the (to be elected) browser master. The next screenshot was taken about one minute later. And it shows even less.

```
[paul@RHEL4b ~]$ smbtree
Password:
WORKGROUP
 \\W2000
[paul@RHEL4b ~]$
```

So we wait a while, and then run **smbtree** again, this time it looks a lot nicer.

```
[paul@RHEL4b ~]$ smbtree
Password:
WORKGROUP
 \\W2000
PEGASUS
 \\WINXP
 \\RHEL4B                        Pegasus Domain Member Server
  \\RHEL4B\ADMIN$                IPC Service (Pegasus Domain Member Server)
  \\RHEL4B\IPC$                  IPC Service (Pegasus Domain Member Server)
  \\RHEL4B\domaindata            Active Directory users only
 \\HM2003
[paul@RHEL4b ~]$ smbtree --version
Version 3.0.10-1.4E.9
[paul@RHEL4b ~]$
```

I added the version number of **smbtree** in the previous screenshot, to show you the difference when using the latest version of smbtree (below a screenshot taken from Ubuntu Feisty Fawn). The latest version shows a more complete overview of machines and shares.

```
paul@laika:~$ smbtree --version
Version 3.0.24
```

```
paul@laika:~$ smbtree
Password:
WORKGROUP
 \\W2000
  \\W2000\firstshare
  \\W2000\C$              Default share
  \\W2000\ADMIN$          Remote Admin
  \\W2000\IPC$            Remote IPC
PEGASUS
 \\WINXP
cli_rpc_pipe_open: cli_nt_create failed on pipe \srvsvc to machine WINXP.
Error was NT_STATUS_ACCESS_DENIED
  \\RHEL4B                       Pegasus Domain Member Server
   \\RHEL4B\ADMIN$               IPC Service (Pegasus Domain Member Server)
   \\RHEL4B\IPC$                 IPC Service (Pegasus Domain Member Server)
   \\RHEL4B\domaindata           Active Directory users only
  \\HM2003
cli_rpc_pipe_open: cli_nt_create failed on pipe \srvsvc to machine HM2003.
Error was NT_STATUS_ACCESS_DENIED
paul@laika:~$
```

The previous screenshot also provides useful errors on why we cannot see shared info on
computers winxp and w2003. Let us try the old **smbtree** version on our RHEL server, but
this time with Administrator credentials (which are the same on all computers).

```
[paul@RHEL4b ~]$ smbtree -UAdministrator%Stargate1
WORKGROUP
 \\W2000
PEGASUS
 \\WINXP
  \\WINXP\C$              Default share
  \\WINXP\ADMIN$          Remote Admin
  \\WINXP\share55
  \\WINXP\IPC$            Remote IPC
  \\RHEL4B                       Pegasus Domain Member Server
   \\RHEL4B\ADMIN$        IPC Service (Pegasus Domain Member Server)
   \\RHEL4B\IPC$          IPC Service (Pegasus Domain Member Server)
   \\RHEL4B\domaindata    Active Directory users only
  \\HM2003
   \\HM2003\NETLOGON      Logon server share
   \\HM2003\SYSVOL        Logon server share
   \\HM2003\WSUSTemp      A network share used by Local Publishing ...
   \\HM2003\ADMIN$        Remote Admin
   \\HM2003\tools
   \\HM2003\IPC$          Remote IPC
   \\HM2003\WsusContent   A network share to be used by Local ...
   \\HM2003\C$            Default share
[paul@RHEL4b ~]$
```

As you can see, this gives a very nice overview of all SMB computers and their shares.

10.5. server string

The comment seen by the **net view** and the **smbclient** commands is the default value for
the **server string** option. Simply adding this value to the global section in **smb.conf** and
restarting samba will change the option.

```
[root@RHEL53 samba]# testparm -s 2>/dev/null | grep server
 server string = Red Hat Server in Paris
```

After a short while, the changed option is visible on the Microsoft computers.

```
C:\Documents and Settings\Administrator>net view
Server Name          Remark

-------------------------------------------------------------------------

\\LAIKA               Ubuntu 9.04 server in Antwerp
\\RHEL53              Red Hat Server in Paris
\\W2003
```

10.6. Samba Web Administration Tool (SWAT)

Samba comes with a web based tool to manage your samba configuration file. **SWAT** is accessible with a web browser on port 901 of the host system. To enable the tool, first find out whether your system is using the **inetd** or the **xinetd** superdaemon.

```
[root@RHEL4b samba]# ps fax | grep inet
 15026 pts/0    S+     0:00                              \_ grep inet
  2771 ?        Ss     0:00 xinetd -stayalive -pidfile /var/run/xinetd.pid
[root@RHEL4b samba]#
```

Then edit the **inetd.conf** or change the disable = yes line in **/etc/xinetd.d/swat** to disable = no.

```
[root@RHEL4b samba]# cat /etc/xinetd.d/swat
# default: off
# description: SWAT is the Samba Web Admin Tool. Use swat \
#               to configure your Samba server. To use SWAT, \
#               connect to port 901 with your favorite web browser.
service swat
{
 port             = 901
 socket_type      = stream
 wait             = no
 only_from        = 127.0.0.1
 user             = root
 server           = /usr/sbin/swat
 log_on_failure  += USERID
 disable          = no
}
[root@RHEL4b samba]# /etc/init.d/xinetd restart
Stopping xinetd:                                          [  OK  ]
Starting xinetd:                                          [  OK  ]
[root@RHEL4b samba]#
```

Change the **only from** value to enable swat from remote computers. This examples shows how to provide swat access to all computers in a /24 subnet.

```
[root@RHEL53 xinetd.d]# grep only /etc/xinetd.d/swat
 only_from  = 192.168.1.0/24
```

Be careful when using SWAT, it erases all your manually edited comments in smb.conf.

10.7. practice: getting started with samba

1. Take a backup copy of the original smb.conf, name it smb.conf.orig

2. Enable SWAT and take a look at it.

3. Stop the Samba server.

4. Create a minimalistic smb.conf.minimal and test it with testparm.

5. Use tesparm -s to create /etc/samba/smb.conf from your smb.conf.minimal .

6. Start Samba with your minimal smb.conf.

7. Verify with smbclient that your Samba server works.

8. Verify that another (Microsoft) computer can see your Samba server.

9. Browse the network with net view, smbtree and with Windows Explorer.

10. Change the "Server String" parameter in smb.conf. How long does it take before you see the change (net view, smbclient, My Network Places,...) ?

11. Will restarting Samba after a change to smb.conf speed up the change ?

12. Which computer is the master browser master in your workgroup ? What is the master browser ?

13. If time permits (or if you are waiting for other students to finish this practice), then install a sniffer (wireshark) and watch the browser elections.

10.8. solution: getting started with samba

1. Take a backup copy of the original smb.conf, name it smb.conf.orig

```
cd /etc/samba ; cp smb.conf smb.conf.orig
```

2. Enable SWAT and take a look at it.

```
on Debian/Ubuntu: vi /etc/inetd.conf (remove # before swat)

on RHEL/Fedora: vi /etc/xinetd.d/swat (set disable to no)
```

3. Stop the Samba server.

```
/etc/init.d/smb stop (Red Hat)

/etc/init.d/samba stop (Debian)
```

4. Create a minimalistic smb.conf.minimal and test it with testparm.

```
cd /etc/samba ; mkdir my_smb_confs ; cd my_smb_confs

vi smb.conf.minimal

testparm smb.conf.minimal
```

5. Use tesparm -s to create /etc/samba/smb.conf from your smb.conf.minimal .

```
testparm -s smb.conf.minimal > ../smb.conf
```

6. Start Samba with your minimal smb.conf.

```
/etc/init.d/smb restart (Red Hat)

/etc/init.d/samba restart (Debian)
```

7. Verify with smbclient that your Samba server works.

```
smbclient -NL 127.0.0.1
```

8. Verify that another computer can see your Samba server.

```
smbclient -NL 'ip-address' (on a Linux)
```

9. Browse the network with net view, smbtree and with Windows Explorer.

```
on Linux: smbtree

on Windows: net view (and WindowsKey + e)
```

10. Change the "Server String" parameter in smb.conf. How long does it take before you see the change (net view, smbclient, My Network Places,...) ?

```
vi /etc/samba/smb.conf

(should take only seconds when restarting samba)
```

11. Will restarting Samba after a change to smb.conf speed up the change ?

```
yes
```

12. Which computer is the master browser master in your workgroup ? What is the master browser ?

```
The computer that won the elections.
```

```
This machine will make the list of computers in the network
```

13. If time permits (or if you are waiting for other students to finish this practice), then install a sniffer (wireshark) and watch the browser elections.

```
On ubuntu: sudo aptitude install wireshark
```

```
then: sudo wireshark, select interface
```

Chapter 11. a read only file server

11.1. Setting up a directory to share

Let's start with setting up a very simple read only file server with Samba. Everyone (even anonymous guests) will receive read access.

The first step is to create a directory and put some test files in it.

```
[root@RHEL52 ~]# mkdir -p /srv/samba/readonly
[root@RHEL52 ~]# cd /srv/samba/readonly/
[root@RHEL52 readonly]# echo "It is cold today." > winter.txt
[root@RHEL52 readonly]# echo "It is hot today." > summer.txt
[root@RHEL52 readonly]# ls -l
total 8
-rw-r--r-- 1 root root 17 Jan 21 05:49 summer.txt
-rw-r--r-- 1 root root 18 Jan 21 05:49 winter.txt
[root@RHEL52 readonly]#
```

11.2. configure the share

11.2.1. smb.conf [global] section

In this example the samba server is a member of WORKGROUP (the default workgroup). We also set a descriptive server string, this string is visible to users browsing the network with net view, windows explorer or smbclient.

```
[root@RHEL52 samba]# head -5 smb.conf
[global]
 workgroup = WORKGROUP
 server string = Public Anonymous File Server
 netbios name = TEACHER0
 security = share
```

You might have noticed the line with **security = share**. This line sets the default security mode for our samba server. Setting the security mode to **share** will allow clients (smbclient, any windows, another Samba server, ...) to provide a password for each share. This is one way of using the SMB/CIFS protocol. The other way (called **user mode**) will allow the client to provide a username/password combination, before the server knows which share the client wants to access.

11.2.2. smb.conf [share] section

The share is called pubread and the path is set to our newly created directory. Everyone is allowed access (**guest ok = yes**) and security is set to read only.

```
[pubread]
path = /srv/samba/readonly
comment = files to read
read only = yes
guest ok = yes
```

Here is a very similar configuration on Ubuntu 11.10.

```
root@ubu1110:~# cat /etc/samba/smb.conf
[global]
workgroup = LINUXTR
netbios name = UBU1110
security = share
[roshare1]
path = /srv/samba/readonly
read only = yes
guest ok = yes
```

It doesn't really matter which Linux distribution you use. Below the same config on Debian 6, as good as identical.

```
root@debian6:~# cat /etc/samba/smb.conf
[global]
workgroup = LINUXTR
netbios name = DEBIAN6
security = share
[roshare1]
path = /srv/samba/readonly
read only = yes
guest ok = yes
```

11.3. restart the server

After testing with **testparm**, restart the samba server (so you don't have to wait).

```
[root@RHEL4b readonly]# service smb restart
Shutting down SMB services:                     [  OK  ]
Shutting down NMB services:                     [  OK  ]
Starting SMB services:                          [  OK  ]
Starting NMB services:                          [  OK  ]
```

11.4. verify the share

11.4.1. verify with smbclient

You can now verify the existence of the share with **smbclient**. Our **pubread** is listed as the fourth share.

```
[root@RHEL52 samba]# smbclient -NL 127.0.0.1
Domain=[WORKGROUP] OS=[Unix] Server=[Samba 3.0.33-3.7.el5]

    Sharename       Type        Comment
    ---------       ----        -------
    IPC$            IPC         IPC Service (Public Anonymous File Server)
    global$         Disk
    pub0            Disk
    pubread         Disk        files to read
Domain=[WORKGROUP] OS=[Unix] Server=[Samba 3.0.33-3.7.el5]

    Server                  Comment
    ---------               -------
    TEACHER0                Samba 3.0.33-3.7.el5
    W2003EE

    Workgroup               Master
    ---------               -------
    WORKGROUP               W2003EE
```

11.4.2. verify on windows

The final test is to go to a Microsoft windows computer and read a file on the Samba server. First we use the **net use** command to mount the pubread share on the driveletter k.

```
C:\>net use K: \\teacher0\pubread
The command completed successfully.
```

Then we test looking at the contents of the share, and reading the files.

```
C:\>dir k:
 Volume in drive K is pubread
 Volume Serial Number is 0C82-11F2

 Directory of K:\

21/01/2009  05:49    <DIR>          .
21/01/2009  05:49    <DIR>          ..
21/01/2009  05:49                17 summer.txt
21/01/2009  05:49                18 winter.txt
               2 File(s)             35 bytes
               2 Dir(s)  13.496.242.176 bytes free
```

Just to be on the safe side, let us try writing.

```
K:\>echo very cold > winter.txt
Access is denied.

K:\>
```

Or you can use windows explorer...

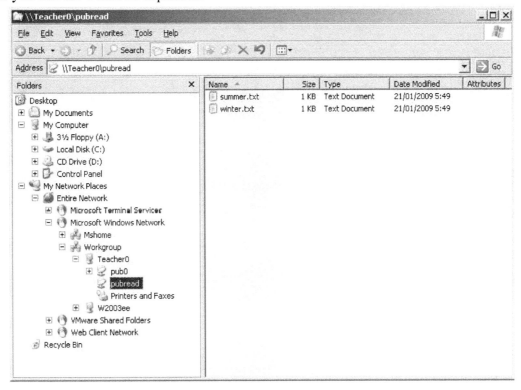

11.5. a note on netcat

The Windows command line screenshot is made in a Linux console, using **netcat** as a pipe to a Windows command shell.

The way this works, is by enabling netcat to listen on the windows computer to a certain port, executing cmd.exe when a connection is received. Netcat is similar to cat, in the way that cat does nothing, only netcat does nothing over the network.

To enable this connection, type the following on the windows computer (after downloading netcat for windows).

```
nc -l -p 23 -t -e cmd.exe
```

And then connect to this machine with netcat from any Linux computer. You end up with a cmd.exe prompt inside your Linux shell.

```
paul@laika:~$ nc 192.168.1.38 23
Microsoft Windows [Version 5.2.3790]
(C) Copyright 1985-2003 Microsoft Corp.

C:\>net use k: /delete
net use k: /delete
k: was deleted successfully.
```

11.6. practice: read only file server

1. Create a directory in a good location (FHS) to share files for everyone to read.

2. Make sure the directory is owned properly and is world accessible.

3. Put a textfile in this directory.

4. Share the directory with Samba.

5. Verify from your own and from another computer (smbclient, net use, ...) that the share is accessible for reading.

6. Make a backup copy of your smb.conf, name it smb.conf.ReadOnlyFileServer.

11.7. solution: read only file server

1. Create a directory in a good location (FHS) to share files for everyone to read.

```
choose one of these...

mkdir -p /srv/samba/readonly

mkdir -p /home/samba/readonly

/home/paul/readonly is wrong!!

/etc/samba/readonly is wrong!!

/readonly is wrong!!
```

2. Make sure the directory is owned properly and is world accessible.

```
chown root:root /srv/samba/readonly

chmod 755 /srv/samba/readonly
```

3. Put a textfile in this directory.

```
echo Hello World > hello.txt
```

4. Share the directory with Samba.

```
You smb.conf.readonly could look like this:
[global]
 workgroup = WORKGROUP
 server string = Read Only File Server
 netbios name = STUDENTx
 security = share

[readonlyX]
 path = /srv/samba/readonly
 comment = read only file share
 read only = yes
 guest ok = yes


test with testparm before going in production!
```

5. Verify from your own and from another computer (smbclient, net use, ...) that the share is accessible for reading.

```
On Linux: smbclient -NL 127.0.0.1

On Windows Explorer: browse to My Network Places

On Windows cmd.exe: net use L: //studentx/readonly
```

6. Make a backup copy of your smb.conf, name it smb.conf.ReadOnlyFileServer.

```
cp smb.conf smb.conf.ReadOnlyFileServer
```

Chapter 12. a writable file server

12.1. set up a directory to share

In this second example, we will create a share where everyone can create files and write to files. Again, we start by creating a directory

```
[root@RHEL52 samba]# mkdir -p /srv/samba/writable
[root@RHEL52 samba]# chmod 777 /srv/samba/writable/
```

12.2. share section in smb.conf

There are two parameters to make a share writable. We can use **read only** or **writable**. This example shows how to use **writable** to give write access to a share.

```
writable = yes
```

And this is an example of using the **read only** parameter to give write access to a share.

```
read only = no
```

12.3. configure the share

Then we simply add a share to our file server by editing **smb.conf**. Below the check with testparm. (We could have changed the description of the server...)

```
[root@RHEL52 samba]# testparm
Load smb config files from /etc/samba/smb.conf
Processing section "[pubwrite]"
Processing section "[pubread]"
Loaded services file OK.
Server role: ROLE_STANDALONE
Press enter to see a dump of your service definitions

[global]
 netbios name = TEACHER0
 server string = Public Anonymous File Server
 security = SHARE

[pubwrite]
 comment = files to write
 path = /srv/samba/writable
 read only = No
 guest ok = Yes

[pubread]
 comment = files to read
 path = /srv/samba/readonly
 guest ok = Yes
```

12.4. test connection with windows

We can now test the connection on a windows 2003 computer. We use the **net use** for this.

```
C:\>net use L: \\teacher0\pubwrite
net use L: \\teacher0\pubwrite
The command completed successfully.
```

12.5. test writing with windows

We mounted the **pubwrite** share on the L: drive in windows. Below we test that we can write to this share.

```
L:\>echo hoi > hoi.txt

L:\>dir
 Volume in drive L is pubwrite
 Volume Serial Number is 0C82-272A

 Directory of L:\

21/01/2009  06:11    <DIR>          .
21/01/2009  06:11    <DIR>          ..
21/01/2009  06:16                 6 hoi.txt
              1 File(s)              6 bytes
              2 Dir(s)  13.496.238.080 bytes free
```

12.6. How is this possible ?

Linux (or any Unix) always needs a user account to gain access to a system. The windows computer did not provide the samba server with a user account or a password. Instead, the Linux owner of the files created through this writable share is the Linux guest account (usually named nobody).

```
[root@RHEL52 samba]# ls -l /srv/samba/writable/
total 4
-rwxr--r-- 1 nobody nobody 6 Jan 21 06:16 hoi.txt
```

So this is not the cleanest solution. We will need to improve this.

12.7. practice: writable file server

1. Create a directory and share it with Samba.

2. Make sure everyone can read and write files, test writing with smbclient and from a Microsoft computer.

3. Verify the ownership of files created by (various) users.

12.8. solution: writable file server

1. Create a directory and share it with Samba.

```
mkdir /srv/samba/writable

chmod 777 /srv/samba/writable


the share section in smb.conf can look like this:

[pubwrite]
 path = /srv/samba/writable
 comment = files to write
 read only = no
 guest ok = yes
```

2. Make sure everyone can read and write files, test writing with smbclient and from a Microsoft computer.

```
to test writing with smbclient:


echo one > count.txt
echo two >> count.txt
echo three >> count.txt
smbclient //localhost/pubwrite
Password:
smb: \> put count.txt
```

3. Verify the ownership of files created by (various) users.

```
ls -l /srv/samba/writable
```

Chapter 13. samba first user account

13.1. creating a samba user

We will create a user for our samba file server and make this user the owner of the directory and all of its files. This anonymous user gets a clear description, but does not get a login shell.

```
[root@RHEL52 samba]# useradd -s /bin/false sambanobody
[root@RHEL52 samba]# usermod -c "Anonymous Samba Access" sambanobody
[root@RHEL52 samba]# passwd sambanobody
Changing password for user sambanobody.
New UNIX password:
Retype new UNIX password:
passwd: all authentication tokens updated successfully.
```

13.2. ownership of files

We can use this user as owner of files and directories, instead of using the root account. This approach is clear and more secure.

```
[root@RHEL52 samba]# chown -R sambanobody:sambanobody /srv/samba/
[root@RHEL52 samba]# ls -al /srv/samba/writable/
total 12
drwxrwxrwx 2 sambanobody sambanobody 4096 Jan 21 06:11 .
drwxr-xr-x 6 sambanobody sambanobody 4096 Jan 21 06:11 ..
-rwxr--r-- 1 sambanobody sambanobody    0 Jan 21 06:16 hoi.txt
```

13.3. /usr/bin/smbpasswd

The sambanobody user account that we created in the previous examples is not yet used by samba. It just owns the files and directories that we created for our shares. The goal of this section is to force ownership of files created through the samba share to belong to our sambanobody user. Remember, our server is still accessible to everyone, nobody needs to know this user account or password. We just want a clean Linux server.

To accomplish this, we first have to tell Samba about this user. We can do this by adding the account to **smbpasswd**.

```
[root@RHEL52 samba]# smbpasswd -a sambanobody
New SMB password:
Retype new SMB password:
Added user sambanobody.
```

13.4. /etc/samba/smbpasswd

To find out where Samba keeps this information (for now), use **smbd -b**. The PRIVATE_DIR variable will show you where the smbpasswd database is located.

```
[root@RHEL52 samba]# smbd -b | grep PRIVATE
   PRIVATE_DIR: /etc/samba
[root@RHEL52 samba]# ls -l smbpasswd
-rw------- 1 root root 110 Jan 21 06:19 smbpasswd
```

You can use a simple cat to see the contents of the **smbpasswd** database. The sambanobody user does have a password (it is secret).

```
[root@RHEL52 samba]# cat smbpasswd
```

```
sambanobody:503:AE9 ... 9DB309C528E540978:[U          ]:LCT-4976B05B:
```

13.5. passdb backend

Note that recent versions of Samba have **tdbsam** as default for the **passdb backend** paramater.

```
root@ubu1110:~# testparm -v 2>/dev/null| grep 'passdb backend'

 passdb backend = tdbsam
```

13.6. forcing this user

Now that Samba knows about this user, we can adjust our writable share to force the ownership of files created through it. For this we use the **force user** and **force group** options. Now we can be sure that all files in the Samba writable share are owned by the same sambanobody user.

Below is the renewed definition of our share in smb.conf.

```
[pubwrite]
 path = /srv/samba/writable
 comment = files to write
 force user = sambanobody
 force group = sambanobody
 read only = no
 guest ok = yes
```

When you reconnect to the share and write a file, then this sambanobody user will own the newly created file (and nobody needs to know the password).

13.7. practice: first samba user account

1. Create a user account for use with samba.

2. Add this user to samba's user database.

3. Create a writable shared directory and use the "force user" and "force group" directives to force ownership of files.

4. Test the working of force user with smbclient, net use and Windows Explorer.

13.8. solution: first samba user account

1. Create a user account for use with samba.

```
useradd -s /bin/false smbguest

usermod -c 'samba guest'

passwd smbguest
```

2. Add this user to samba's user database.

```
smbpasswd -a smbguest
```

3. Create a writable shared directory and use the "force user" and "force group" directives to force ownership of files.

```
[userwrite]
 path = /srv/samba/userwrite
 comment = everyone writes files owned by smbguest
 read only = no
 guest ok = yes
 force user = smbguest
 force group = smbguest
```

4. Test the working of force user with smbclient, net use and Windows Explorer.

```
ls -l /srv/samba/userwrite (and verify ownership)
```

Chapter 14. samba authentication

14.1. creating the users on Linux

The goal of this example is to set up a file share accessible to a number of different users. The users will need to authenticate with their password before access to this share is granted. We will first create three randomly named users, each with their own password. First we add these users to Linux.

```
[root@RHEL52 ~]# useradd -c "Serena Williams" serena
[root@RHEL52 ~]# useradd -c "Justine Henin" justine
[root@RHEL52 ~]# useradd -c "Martina Hingis" martina
[root@RHEL52 ~]# passwd serena
Changing password for user serena.
New UNIX password:
Retype new UNIX password:
passwd: all authentication tokens updated successfully.
[root@RHEL52 ~]# passwd justine
Changing password for user justine.
New UNIX password:
Retype new UNIX password:
passwd: all authentication tokens updated successfully.
[root@RHEL52 ~]# passwd martina
Changing password for user martina.
New UNIX password:
Retype new UNIX password:
passwd: all authentication tokens updated successfully.
```

14.2. creating the users on samba

Then we add them to the **smbpasswd** file, with the same password.

```
[root@RHEL52 ~]# smbpasswd -a serena
New SMB password:
Retype new SMB password:
Added user serena.
[root@RHEL52 ~]# smbpasswd -a justine
New SMB password:
Retype new SMB password:
Added user justine.
[root@RHEL52 ~]# smbpasswd -a martina
New SMB password:
Retype new SMB password:
Added user martina.
```

14.3. security = user

Remember that we set samba's security mode to share with the **security = share** directive in the [global] section ? Since we now require users to always provide a userid and password for access to our samba server, we will need to change this. Setting **security = user** will require the client to provide samba with a valid userid and password before giving access to a share.

Our [global] section now looks like this.

```
[global]
 workgroup = WORKGROUP
 netbios name = TEACHER0
 server string = Samba File Server
 security = user
```

14.4. configuring the share

We add the following [share] section to our smb.conf (and we do not forget to create the directory /srv/samba/authwrite).

```
[authwrite]
path = /srv/samba/authwrite
comment = authenticated users only
read only = no
guest ok = no
```

14.5. testing access with net use

After restarting samba, we test with different users from within Microsoft computers. The screenshots use the **net use**First serena from Windows XP.

```
C:\>net use m: \\teacher0\authwrite stargate /user:serena
The command completed successfully.

C:\>m:

M:\>echo greetings from Serena > serena.txt
```

The next screenshot is martina on a Windows 2000 computer, she succeeds in writing her files, but fails to overwrite the file from serena.

```
C:\>net use k: \\teacher0\authwrite stargate /user:martina
The command completed successfully.

C:\>k:

K:\>echo greetings from martina > Martina.txt

K:\>echo test overwrite > serena.txt
Access is denied.
```

14.6. testing access with smbclient

You can also test connecting with authentication with **smbclient**. First we test with a wrong password.

```
[root@RHEL52 samba]# smbclient //teacher0/authwrite -U martina wrongpass
session setup failed: NT_STATUS_LOGON_FAILURE
```

Then we test with the correct password, and verify that we can access a file on the share.

```
[root@RHEL52 samba]# smbclient //teacher0/authwrite -U martina stargate
Domain=[TEACHER0] OS=[Unix] Server=[Samba 3.0.33-3.7.el5]
smb: \> more serena.txt
getting file \serena.txt of size 14 as /tmp/smbmore.QQfmSN (6.8 kb/s)
one
two
three
smb: \> q
```

14.7. verify ownership

We now have a simple standalone samba file server with authenticated access. And the files in the shares belong to their proper owners.

```
[root@RHEL52 samba]# ls -l /srv/samba/authwrite/
total 8
-rwxr--r-- 1 martina martina  0 Jan 21 20:06 martina.txt
-rwxr--r-- 1 serena  serena  14 Jan 21 20:06 serena.txt
-rwxr--r-- 1 serena  serena   6 Jan 21 20:09 ser.txt
```

14.8. common problems

14.8.1. NT_STATUS_BAD_NETWORK_NAME

You can get **NT_STATUS_BAD_NETWORK_NAME** when you forget to create the target directory.

```
[root@RHEL52 samba]# rm -rf /srv/samba/authwrite/
[root@RHEL52 samba]# smbclient //teacher0/authwrite -U martina stargate
Domain=[TEACHER0] OS=[Unix] Server=[Samba 3.0.33-3.7.el5]
tree connect failed: NT_STATUS_BAD_NETWORK_NAME
```

14.8.2. NT_STATUS_LOGON_FAILURE

You can get **NT_STATUS_LOGON_FAILURE** when you type the wrong password or when you type an unexisting username.

```
[root@RHEL52 samba]# smbclient //teacher0/authwrite -U martina STARGATE
session setup failed: NT_STATUS_LOGON_FAILURE
```

14.8.3. usernames are (not) case sensitive

Remember that usernames om Linux are case sensitive.

```
[root@RHEL52 samba]# su - MARTINA
su: user MARTINA does not exist
```

```
[root@RHEL52 samba]# su - martina
[martina@RHEL52 ~]$
```

But usernames on Microsoft computers are not case sensitive.

```
[root@RHEL52 samba]# smbclient //teacher0/authwrite -U martina stargate
Domain=[TEACHER0] OS=[Unix] Server=[Samba 3.0.33-3.7.el5]
smb: \> q
[root@RHEL52 samba]# smbclient //teacher0/authwrite -U MARTINA stargate
Domain=[TEACHER0] OS=[Unix] Server=[Samba 3.0.33-3.7.el5]
smb: \> q
```

14.9. practice : samba authentication

0. Make sure you have properly named backups of your smb.conf of the previous practices.

1. Create three users (on the Linux and on the samba), remember their passwords!

2. Set up a shared directory that is only accessible to authenticated users.

3. Use smbclient and a windows computer to access your share, use more than one user account (windows requires a logoff/logon for this).

4. Verify that files created by these users belong to them.

5. Try to change or delete a file from another user.

14.10. solution: samba authentication

1. Create three users (on the Linux and on the samba), remember their passwords!

```
useradd -c 'SMB user1' userx
```

```
passwd userx
```

2. Set up a shared directory that is only accessible to authenticated users.

```
The shared section in smb.conf could look like this:
```

```
[authwrite]
 path = /srv/samba/authwrite
 comment = authenticated users only
 read only = no
 guest ok = no
```

3. Use smbclient and a windows computer to access your share, use more than one user account (windows requires a logoff/logon for this).

```
on Linux: smbclient //studentX/authwrite -U user1 password
```

```
on windows net use p: \\studentX\authwrite password /user:user2
```

4. Verify that files created by these users belong to them.

```
ls -l /srv/samba/authwrite
```

5. Try to change or delete a file from another user.

```
you should not be able to change or overwrite files from others.
```

Chapter 15. samba securing shares

15.1. security based on user name

15.1.1. valid users

To restrict users per share, you can use the **valid users** parameter. In the example below, only the users listed as valid will be able to access the tennis share.

```
[tennis]
 path = /srv/samba/tennis
 comment = authenticated and valid users only
 read only = No
 guest ok = No
 valid users = serena, kim, venus, justine
```

15.1.2. invalid users

If you are paranoia, you can also use **invalid users** to explicitely deny the listed users access. When a user is in both lists, the user has no access!

```
[tennis]
 path = /srv/samba/tennis
 read only = No
 guest ok = No
 valid users = kim, serena, venus, justine
 invalid users = venus
```

15.1.3. read list

On a writable share, you can set a list of read only users with the **read list** parameter.

```
[football]
 path = /srv/samba/football
 read only = No
 guest ok = No
 read list = martina, roberto
```

15.1.4. write list

Even on a read only share, you can set a list of users that can write. Use the **write list** parameter.

```
[football]
 path = /srv/samba/golf
 read only = Yes
 guest ok = No
 write list = eddy, jan
```

15.2. security based on ip-address

15.2.1. hosts allow

The **hosts allow** or **allow hosts** parameter is one of the key advantages of Samba. It allows access control of shares on the ip-address level. To allow only specific hosts to access a share, list the hosts, separated by comma's.

```
allow hosts = 192.168.1.5, 192.168.1.40
```

Allowing entire subnets is done by ending the range with a dot.

```
allow hosts = 192.168.1.
```

Subnet masks can be added in the classical way.

```
allow hosts = 10.0.0.0/255.0.0.0
```

You can also allow an entire subnet with exceptions.

```
hosts allow = 10. except 10.0.0.12
```

15.2.2. hosts deny

The **hosts deny** or **deny hosts** parameter is the logical counterpart of the previous. The syntax is the same as for hosts allow.

```
hosts deny = 192.168.1.55, 192.168.1.56
```

15.3. security through obscurity

15.3.1. hide unreadable

Setting **hide unreadable** to yes will prevent users from seeing files that cannot be read by them.

```
hide unreadable = yes
```

15.3.2. browsable

Setting the **browseable = no** directive will hide shares from My Network Places. But it will not prevent someone from accessing the share (when the name of the share is known).

Note that **browsable** and **browseable** are both correct syntax.

```
[pubread]
 path = /srv/samba/readonly
 comment = files to read
 read only = yes
 guest ok = yes
 browseable = no
```

15.4. file system security

15.4.1. create mask

You can use **create mask** and **directory mask** to set the maximum allowed permissions for newly created files and directories. The mask you set is an AND mask (it takes permissions away).

```
[tennis]
 path = /srv/samba/tennis
 read only = No
```

```
guest ok = No
create mask = 640
directory mask = 750
```

15.4.2. force create mode

Similar to **create mask**, but different. Where the mask from above was a logical AND, the mode you set here is a logical OR (so it adds permissions). You can use the **force create mode** and **force directory mode** to set the minimal required permissions for newly created files and directories.

```
[tennis]
path = /srv/samba/tennis
read only = No
guest ok = No
force create mode = 444
force directory mode = 550
```

15.4.3. security mask

The **security mask** and **directory security mask** work in the same way as **create mask** and **directory mask**, but apply only when a windows user is changing permissions using the windows security dialog box.

15.4.4. force security mode

The **force security mode** and **force directory security mode** work in the same way as **force create mode** and **force directory mode**, but apply only when a windows user is changing permissions using the windows security dialog box.

15.4.5. inherit permissions

With **inherit permissions** = **yes** you can force newly created files and directories to inherit permissions from their parent directory, overriding the create mask and directory mask settings.

```
[authwrite]
path = /srv/samba/authwrite
comment = authenticated users only
read only = no
guest ok = no
create mask = 600
directory mask = 555
inherit permissions = yes
```

15.5. practice: securing shares

1. Create a writable share called sales, and a readonly share called budget. Test that it works.

2. Limit access to the sales share to ann, sandra and veronique.

3. Make sure that roberto cannot access the sales share.

4. Even though the sales share is writable, ann should only have read access.

5. Even though the budget share is read only, sandra should also have write access.

6. Limit one shared directory to the 192.168.1.0/24 subnet, and another share to the two computers with ip-addresses 192.168.1.33 and 172.17.18.19.

7. Make sure the computer with ip 192.168.1.203 cannot access the budget share.

8. Make sure (on the budget share) that users can see only files and directories to which they have access.

9. Make sure the sales share is not visible when browsing the network.

10. All files created in the sales share should have 640 permissions or less.

11. All directories created in the budget share should have 750 permissions or more.

12. Permissions for files on the sales share should never be set more than 664.

13. Permissions for files on the budget share should never be set less than 500.

14. If time permits (or if you are waiting for other students to finish this practice), then combine the "read only" and "writable" statements to check which one has priority.

15. If time permits then combine "read list", "write list", "hosts allow" and "hosts deny". Which of these has priority ?

15.6. solution: securing shares

1. Create a writable share called sales, and a readonly share called budget. Test that it works.

```
see previous solutions on how to do this...
```

2. Limit access to the sales share to ann, sandra and veronique.

```
valid users = ann, sandra, veronique
```

3. Make sure that roberto cannot access the sales share.

```
invalid users = roberto
```

4. Even though the sales share is writable, ann should only have read access.

```
read list = ann
```

5. Even though the budget share is read only, sandra should also have write access.

```
write list = sandra
```

6. Limit one shared directory to the 192.168.1.0/24 subnet, and another share to the two computers with ip-addresses 192.168.1.33 and 172.17.18.19.

```
hosts allow = 192.168.1.

hosts allow = 192.168.1.33, 172.17.18.19
```

7. Make sure the computer with ip 192.168.1.203 cannot access the budget share.

```
hosts deny = 192.168.1.203
```

8. Make sure (on the budget share) that users can see only files and directories to which they have access.

```
hide unreadable = yes
```

9. Make sure the sales share is not visible when browsing the network.

```
browsable = no
```

10. All files created in the sales share should have 640 permissions or less.

```
create mask = 640
```

11. All directories created in the budget share should have 750 permissions or more.

```
force directory mode = 750
```

12. Permissions for files on the sales share should never be set more than 664.

```
security mask = 750
```

13. Permissions for files on the budget share should never be set less than 500.

```
force security directory mask = 500
```

14. If time permits (or if you are waiting for other students to finish this practice), then combine the "read only" and "writable" statements to check which one has priority.

15. If time permits then combine "read list", "write list", "hosts allow" and "hosts deny". Which of these has priority ?

Chapter 16. samba domain member

16.1. changes in smb.conf

16.1.1. workgroup

The **workgroup** option in the global section should match the netbios name of the Active Directory domain.

```
workgroup = STARGATE
```

16.1.2. security mode

Authentication will not be handled by samba now, but by the Active Directory domain controllers, so we set the **security** option to domain.

```
security = Domain
```

16.1.3. Linux uid's

Linux requires a user account for every user accessing its file system, we need to provide Samba with a range of uid's and gid's that it can use to create these user accounts. The range is determined with the **idmap uid** and the **idmap gid** parameters. The first Active Directory user to connect will receive Linux uid 20000.

```
idmap uid = 20000-22000
idmap gid = 20000-22000
```

16.1.4. winbind use default domain

The **winbind use default domain** parameter makes sure winbind also operates on users without a domain component in their name.

```
winbind use default domain = yes
```

16.1.5. [global] section in smb.conf

Below is our new global section in **smb.conf**.

```
[global]
 workgroup = STARGATE
 security = Domain
 server string = Stargate Domain Member Server
 idmap uid = 20000-22000
 idmap gid = 20000-22000
 winbind use default domain = yes
```

16.1.6. realm in /etc/krb5.conf

To connect to a Windows 2003 sp2 (or later) you will need to adjust the kerberos realm in **/etc/krb5.conf** and set both lookup statements to true.

```
[libdefaults]
 default_realm = STARGATE.LOCAL
 dns_lookup_realm = true
 dns_lookup_kdc = true
```

16.1.7. [share] section in smb.conf

Nothing special is required for the share section in smb.conf. Remember that we do not manually create users in smbpasswd or on the Linux (/etc/passwd). Only Active Directory users are allowed access.

```
[domaindata]
 path = /srv/samba/domaindata
 comment = Active Directory users only
 read only = No
```

16.2. joining an Active Directory domain

While the Samba server is stopped, you can use **net rpc join** to join the Active Directory domain.

```
[root@RHEL52 samba]# service smb stop
Shutting down SMB services:                               [  OK  ]
Shutting down NMB services:                               [  OK  ]
[root@RHEL52 samba]# net rpc join -U Administrator
Password:
Joined domain STARGATE.
```

We can verify in the aduc (Active Directory Users and Computers) that a computer account is created for this samba server.

16.3. winbind

16.3.1. adding winbind to nsswitch.conf

The **winbind daemon** is talking with the Active Directory domain.

We need to update the **/etc/nsswitch.conf** file now, so user group and host names can be resolved against the winbind daemon.

```
[root@RHEL52 samba]# vi /etc/nsswitch.conf
[root@RHEL52 samba]# grep winbind /etc/nsswitch.conf
passwd:     files winbind
group:      files winbind
hosts:      files dns winbind
```

16.3.2. starting samba and winbindd

Time to start Samba followed by **winbindd**.

```
[root@RHEL4b samba]# service smb start
Starting SMB services:                              [  OK  ]
Starting NMB services:                              [  OK  ]
[root@RHEL4b samba]# service winbind start
Starting winbindd services:                         [  OK  ]
[root@RHEL4b samba]#
```

16.4. wbinfo

16.4.1. verify the trust

You can use **wbinfo -t** to verify the trust between your samba server and Active Directory.

```
[root@RHEL52 ~]# wbinfo -t
checking the trust secret via RPC calls succeeded
```

16.4.2. list all users

We can obtain a list of all user with the **wbinfo -u** command. The domain is not shown when the **winbind use default domain** parameter is set.

```
[root@RHEL52 ~]# wbinfo -u
TEACHER0\serena
TEACHER0\justine
TEACHER0\martina
STARGATE\administrator
STARGATE\guest
STARGATE\support_388945a0
STARGATE\pol
STARGATE\krbtgt
STARGATE\arthur
STARGATE\harry
```

16.4.3. list all groups

We can obtain a list of all domain groups with the **wbinfo -g** command. The domain is not shown when the **winbind use default domain** parameter is set.

```
[root@RHEL52 ~]# wbinfo -g
BUILTIN\administrators
BUILTIN\users
BATMAN\domain computers
BATMAN\domain controllers
BATMAN\schema admins
BATMAN\enterprise admins
BATMAN\domain admins
BATMAN\domain users
BATMAN\domain guests
BATMAN\group policy creator owners
BATMAN\dnsupdateproxy
```

16.4.4. query a user

We can use **wbinfo -a** to verify authentication of a user against Active Directory. Assuming a user account **harry** with password **stargate** is just created on the Active Directory, we get the following screenshot.

```
[root@RHEL52 ~]# wbinfo -a harry%stargate
plaintext password authentication succeeded
challenge/response password authentication succeeded
```

16.5. getent

We can use **getent** to verify that winbindd is working and actually adding the Active directory users to /etc/passwd.

```
[root@RHEL52 ~]# getent passwd harry
harry:*:20000:20008:harry potter:/home/BATMAN/harry:/bin/false
[root@RHEL52 ~]# getent passwd arthur
arthur:*:20001:20008:arthur dent:/home/BATMAN/arthur:/bin/false
[root@RHEL52 ~]# getent passwd bilbo
bilbo:*:20002:20008:bilbo baggins:/home/BATMAN/bilbo:/bin/false
```

If the user already exists locally, then the local user account is shown. This is because winbind is configured in **/etc/nsswitch.conf** after **files**.

```
[root@RHEL52 ~]# getent passwd paul
paul:x:500:500:Paul Cobbaut:/home/paul:/bin/bash
```

All the Active Directory users can now easily connect to the Samba share. Files created by them, belong to them.

16.6. file ownership

```
[root@RHEL4b samba]# ll /srv/samba/domaindata/
total 0
-rwxr--r-- 1 justine 20000 0 Jun 22 19:54 create_by_justine_on_winxp.txt
-rwxr--r-- 1 venus   20000 0 Jun 22 19:55 create_by_venus.txt
-rwxr--r-- 1 maria   20000 0 Jun 22 19:57 Maria.txt
```

16.7. practice : samba domain member

1. Verify that you have a working Active Directory (AD) domain.

2. Add the domain name and domain controller to /etc/hosts. Set the AD-DNS in /etc/resolv.conf.

3. Setup Samba as a member server in the domain.

4. Verify the creation of a computer account in AD for your Samba server.

5. Verify the automatic creation of AD users in /etc/passwd with wbinfo and getent.

6. Connect to Samba shares with AD users, and verify ownership of their files.

Chapter 17. samba domain controller

17.1. about Domain Controllers

17.1.1. Windows NT4

Windows NT4 works with single master replication domain controllers. There is exactly one PDC (Primary Domain Controller) in the domain, and zero or more BDC's (Backup Domain Controllers). Samba 3 has all features found in Windows NT4 PDC and BDC, and more. This includes file and print serving, domain control with single logon, logon scripts, home directories and roaming profiles.

17.1.2. Windows 200x

With Windows 2000 came Active Directory. AD includes multimaster replication and group policies. Samba 3 can only be a member server in Active Directory, it cannot manage group policies. Samba 4 can do this (in beta).

17.1.3. Samba 3

Samba 3 can act as a domain controller in its own domain. In a Windows NT4 domain, with one Windows NT4 PDC and zero or more BDC's, Samba 3 can only be a member server. The same is valid for Samba 3 in an Active Directory Domain. In short, a Samba 3 domain controller can not share domain control with Windows domain controllers.

17.1.4. Samba 4

Samba 4 can be a domain controller in an Active Directory domain, including managing group policies. As of this writing, Samba 4 is not released for production!

17.2. About security modes

17.2.1. security = share

The 'Windows for Workgroups' way of working, a client requests connection to a share and provides a password for that connection. Aanyone who knows a password for a share can access that share. This security model was common in Windows 3.11, Windows 95, Windows 98 and Windows ME.

17.2.2. security = user

The client will send a userid + password before the server knows which share the client wants to access. This mode should be used whenever the samba server is in control of the user database. Both for standalone and samba domain controllers.

17.2.3. security = domain

This mode will allow samba to verify user credentials using NTLM in Windows NT4 and in all Active Directory domains. This is similar to Windows NT4 BDC's joining a native Windows 2000/3 Active Directory domain.

17.2.4. security = ads

This mode will make samba use Kerberos to connect to the Active Directory domain.

17.2.5. security = server

This mode is obsolete, it can be used to forward authentication to another server.

17.3. About password backends

The previous chapters all used the **smbpasswd** user database. For domain control we opt for the **tdbsam** password backend. Another option would be to use LDAP. Larger domains will benefit from using LDAP instead of the not so scalable tdbsam. When you need more than one Domain Controller, then the Samba team advises to not use tdbsam.

17.4. [global] section in smb.conf

Now is a good time to start adding comments in your smb.conf. First we will take a look at the naming of our domain and server in the **[global]** section, and at the domain controlling parameters.

17.4.1. security

The security must be set to user (which is the default). This mode will make samba control the user accounts, so it will allow samba to act as a domain controller.

```
security = user
```

17.4.2. os level

A samba server is the most stable computer in the network, so it should win all browser elections (**os level** above 32) to become the **browser master**

```
os level = 33
```

17.4.3. passdb backend

The **passdb backend** parameter will determine whether samba uses **smbpasswd**, **tdbsam** or ldap.

```
passdb backend = tdbsam
```

17.4.4. preferred master

Setting the **preferred master** parameter to yes will make the nmbd daemon force an election on startup.

```
preferred master = yes
```

17.4.5. domain logons

Setting the **domain logons** parameter will make this samba server a domain controller.

```
domain logons = yes
```

17.4.6. domain master

Setting the **domain master** parameter can cause samba to claim the **domain master browser** role for its workgroup. Don't use this parameter in a workgroup with an active NT4 PDC.

```
domain master = yes
```

17.4.7. [global] section

The screenshot below shows a sample [global] section for a samba domain controller.

```
[global]
# names
 workgroup = SPORTS
 netbios name = DCSPORTS
 server string = Sports Domain Controller
# domain control parameters
 security = user
 os level = 33
 preferred master = Yes
 domain master = Yes
 domain logons = Yes
```

17.5. netlogon share

Part of the microsoft definition for a domain controller is that it should have a **netlogon share**. This is the relevant part of smb.conf to create this netlogon share on Samba.

```
[netlogon]
comment = Network Logon Service
path = /srv/samba/netlogon
admin users = root
guest ok = Yes
browseable = No
```

17.6. other [share] sections

We create some sections for file shares, to test the samba server. Users can all access the general sports file share, but only group members can access their own sports share.

```
[sports]
comment = Information about all sports
path = /srv/samba/sports
valid users = @ntsports
read only = No

[tennis]
comment = Information about tennis
path = /srv/samba/tennis
valid users = @nttennis
read only = No
```

```
[football]
comment = Information about football
path = /srv/samba/football
valid users = @ntfootball
read only = No
```

17.7. Users and Groups

To be able to use users and groups in the samba domain controller, we can first set up some groups on the Linux computer.

```
[root@RHEL52 samba]# groupadd ntadmins
[root@RHEL52 samba]# groupadd ntsports
[root@RHEL52 samba]# groupadd ntfootball
[root@RHEL52 samba]# groupadd nttennis
```

This enables us to add group membership info to some new users for our samba domain. Don't forget to give them a password.

```
[root@RHEL52 samba]# useradd -m -G ntadmins Administrator
[root@RHEL52 samba]# useradd -m -G ntsports,nttennis venus
[root@RHEL52 samba]# useradd -m -G ntsports,nttennis kim
[root@RHEL52 samba]# useradd -m -G ntsports,nttennis jelena
[root@RHEL52 samba]# useradd -m -G ntsports,ntfootball figo
[root@RHEL52 samba]# useradd -m -G ntsports,ntfootball ronaldo
[root@RHEL52 samba]# useradd -m -G ntsports,ntfootball pfaff
```

It is always safe to verify creation of users, groups and passwords in /etc/passwd, /etc/shadow and /etc/group.

```
[root@RHEL52 samba]# tail -11 /etc/group
ntadmins:x:507:Administrator
ntsports:x:508:venus,kim,jelena,figo,ronaldo,pfaff
ntfootball:x:509:figo,ronaldo,pfaff
nttennis:x:510:venus,kim,jelena
Administrator:x:511:
venus:x:512:
kim:x:513:
jelena:x:514:
figo:x:515:
ronaldo:x:516:
pfaff:x:517:
```

17.8. tdbsam

Next we must make these users known to samba with the smbpasswd tool. When you add the first user to **tdbsam**, the file **/etc/samba/passdb.tdb** will be created.

```
[root@RHEL52 samba]# smbpasswd -a root
New SMB password:
```

```
Retype new SMB password:
tdbsam_open: Converting version 0 database to version 3.
Added user root.
```

Adding all the other users generates less output, because tdbsam is already created.

```
[root@RHEL4b samba]# smbpasswd -a root
New SMB password:
Retype new SMB password:
Added user root.
```

17.9. about computer accounts

Every NT computer (Windows NT, 2000, XP, Vista) can become a member of a domain. Joining the domain (by right-clicking on My Computer) means that a computer account will be created in the domain. This computer account also has a password (but you cannot know it) to prevent other computers with the same name from accidentally becoming member of the domain. The computer account created by Samba is visible in the **/etc/passwd** file on Linux. Computer accounts appear as a normal user account, but end their name with a dollar sign. Below a screenshot of the windows 2003 computer account, created by Samba 3.

```
[root@RHEL52 samba]# tail -5 /etc/passwd
jelena:x:510:514::/home/jelena:/bin/bash
figo:x:511:515::/home/figo:/bin/bash
ronaldo:x:512:516::/home/ronaldo:/bin/bash
pfaff:x:513:517::/home/pfaff:/bin/bash
w2003ee$:x:514:518::/home/nobody:/bin/false
```

To be able to create the account, you will need to provide credentials of an account with the permission to create accounts (by default only root can do this on Linux). And we will have to tell Samba how to to this, by adding an **add machine script** to the global section of smb.conf.

```
add machine script = /usr/sbin/useradd -s /bin/false -d /home/nobody %u
```

You can now join a Microsoft computer to the sports domain (with the root user). After reboot of the Microsoft computer, you will be able to logon with Administrator (password Stargate1), but you will get an error about your roaming profile. We will fix this in the next section.

When joining the samba domain, you have to enter the credentials of a Linux account that can create users (usually only root can do this). If the Microsoft computer complains with **The parameter is incorrect**, then you possibly forgot to add the **add machine script**.

17.10. local or roaming profiles

For your information, if you want to force local profiles instead of roaming profiles, then simply add the following two lines to the global section in smb.conf.

```
logon home =
logon path =
```

Microsoft computers store a lot of User Metadata and application data in a user profile. Making this profile available on the network will enable users to keep their Desktop and Application settings across computers. User profiles on the network are called **roaming profiles** or **roving profiles**. The Samba domain controller can manage these profiles. First we need to add the relevant section in smb.conf.

```
[Profiles]
 comment = User Profiles
 path = /srv/samba/profiles
 readonly = No
 profile acls = Yes
```

Besides the share section, we also need to set the location of the profiles share (this can be another Samba server) in the global section.

```
logon path = \\%L\Profiles\%U
```

The **%L** variable is the name of this Samba server, the **%U** variable translates to the username. After adding a user to smbpasswd and letting the user log on and off, the profile of the user will look like this.

```
[root@RHEL4b samba]# ll /srv/samba/profiles/Venus/
total 568
drwxr-xr-x  4 Venus Venus   4096 Jul  5 10:03 Application Data
drwxr-xr-x  2 Venus Venus   4096 Jul  5 10:03 Cookies
drwxr-xr-x  3 Venus Venus   4096 Jul  5 10:03 Desktop
drwxr-xr-x  3 Venus Venus   4096 Jul  5 10:03 Favorites
drwxr-xr-x  4 Venus Venus   4096 Jul  5 10:03 My Documents
drwxr-xr-x  2 Venus Venus   4096 Jul  5 10:03 NetHood
-rwxr--r--  1 Venus Venus 524288 Jul  5  2007 NTUSER.DAT
-rwxr--r--  1 Venus Venus   1024 Jul  5  2007 NTUSER.DAT.LOG
-rw-r--r--  1 Venus Venus    268 Jul  5 10:03 ntuser.ini
drwxr-xr-x  2 Venus Venus   4096 Jul  5 10:03 PrintHood
drwxr-xr-x  2 Venus Venus   4096 Jul  5 10:03 Recent
drwxr-xr-x  2 Venus Venus   4096 Jul  5 10:03 SendTo
drwxr-xr-x  3 Venus Venus   4096 Jul  5 10:03 Start Menu
drwxr-xr-x  2 Venus Venus   4096 Jul  5 10:03 Templates
```

17.11. Groups in NTFS acls

We have users on Unix, we have groups on Unix that contain those users.

```
[root@RHEL4b samba]# grep nt /etc/group
...
ntadmins:x:506:Administrator
ntsports:x:507:Venus,Serena,Kim,Figo,Pfaff
nttennis:x:508:Venus,Serena,Kim
ntfootball:x:509:Figo,Pfaff
```

```
[root@RHEL4b samba]#
```

We already added Venus to the **tdbsam** with **smbpasswd**.

```
smbpasswd -a Venus
```

Does this mean that Venus can access the tennis and the sports shares ? Yes, all access works fine on the Samba server. But the nttennis group is not available on the windows machines. To make the groups available on windows (like in the ntfs security tab of files and folders), we have to map unix groups to windows groups. To do this, we use the **net groupmap** command.

```
[root@RHEL4b samba]# net groupmap add ntgroup="tennis" unixgroup=nttennis type=d
No rid or sid specified, choosing algorithmic mapping
Successully added group tennis to the mapping db
[root@RHEL4b samba]# net groupmap add ntgroup="football" unixgroup=ntfootball type=d
No rid or sid specified, choosing algorithmic mapping
Successully added group football to the mapping db
[root@RHEL4b samba]# net groupmap add ntgroup="sports" unixgroup=ntsports type=d
No rid or sid specified, choosing algorithmic mapping
Successully added group sports to the mapping db
[root@RHEL4b samba]#
```

Now you can use the Samba groups on all NTFS volumes on members of the domain.

17.12. logon scripts

Before testing a logon script, make sure it has the proper carriage returns that DOS files have.

```
[root@RHEL4b netlogon]# cat start.bat
net use Z: \\DCSPORTS0\SPORTS
[root@RHEL4b netlogon]# unix2dos start.bat
unix2dos: converting file start.bat to DOS format ...
[root@RHEL4b netlogon]#
```

Then copy the scripts to the netlogon share, and add the following parameter to smb.conf.

```
logon script = start.bat
```

17.13. practice: samba domain controller

1. Setup Samba as a domain controller.

2. Create the shares salesdata, salespresentations and meetings. Salesdata must be accessible to all sales people and to all managers. SalesPresentations is only for all sales people. Meetings is only accessible to all managers. Use groups to accomplish this.

3. Join a Microsoft computer to your domain. Verify the creation of a computer account in /etc/passwd.

4. Setup and verify the proper working of roaming profiles.

5. Find information about home directories for users, set them up and verify that users receive their home directory mapped under the H:-drive in MS Windows Explorer.

6. Use a couple of samba domain groups with members to set acls on ntfs. Verify that it works!

7. Knowing that the %m variable contains the computername, create a separate log file for every computer(account).

8. Knowing that %s contains the client operating system, include a smb.%s.conf file that contains a share. (The share will only be visible to clients with that OS).

9. If time permits (or if you are waiting for other students to finish this practice), then combine "valid users" and "invalid users" with groups and usernames with "hosts allow" and "hosts deny" and make a table of which get priority over which.

Chapter 18. a brief look at samba 4

18.1. Samba 4 alpha 6

A quick view on Samba 4 alpha 6 (January 2009). You can also follow this guide http://wiki.samba.org/index.php/Samba4/HOWTO

Remove old Samba from Red Hat

```
yum remove samba
```

set a fix ip address (Red Hat has an easy GUI)

download and untar

```
samba.org, click 'download info', choose mirror, dl samba4 latest alpha
```

once untarred, enter the directory and read the howto4.txt

```
cd samba-4.0.0alpha6/
```

```
more howto4.txt
```

first we have to configure, compile and install samba4

```
cd source4/
```

```
./configure
```

```
make
```

```
make install
```

Then we can use the provision script to setup our realm. I used booi.schot as domain name (instead of example.com).

```
./setup/provision --realm=BOOI.SCHOT --domain=BOOI --adminpass=stargate \
--server-role='domain controller'
```

i added a simple share for testing

```
vi /usr/local/samba/etc/smb.conf
```

then i started samba

```
cd /usr/local/samba/sbin/
```

```
./samba
```

I tested with smbclient, it works

```
smbclient //localhost/test -Uadministrator%stargate
```

I checked that bind (and bind-chroot) were installed (yes), so copied the srv records

```
cp booi.schot.zone /var/named/chroot/etc/
```

then appended to named.conf

```
cat named.conf >> /var/named/chroot/etc/named.conf
```

I followed these steps in the howto4.txt

```
vi /etc/init.d/named   [added two export lines right after start()]
chmod a+r /usr/local/samba/private/dns.keytab
cp krb5.conf /etc/
vi /var/named/chroot/etc/named.conf
 --> remove a lot, but keep allow-update { any; };
```

restart bind (named!), then tested dns with dig, this works (stripped screenshot!)

```
[root@RHEL52 private]# dig _ldap._tcp.dc._msdcs.booi.schot SRV @localhost

; (1 server found)
;; global options:  printcmd
;; Got answer:
;; -HEADER- opcode: QUERY, status: NXDOMAIN, id: 58186
;; flags: qr rd ra; QUERY: 1, ANSWER: 0, AUTHORITY: 1, ADDITIONAL: 0

;; QUESTION SECTION:
;_ldap._tcp.dc._msdcs.booi.schot. IN SRV

;; AUTHORITY SECTION:
.    10800 IN SOA A.ROOT-SERVERS.NET....

;; Query time: 54 msec
;; SERVER: 127.0.0.1#53(127.0.0.1)
;; WHEN: Tue Jan 27 20:57:05 2009
;; MSG SIZE  rcvd: 124

[root@RHEL52 private]#
```

made sure /etc/resolv.conf points to himself

```
[root@RHEL52 private]# cat /etc/resolv.conf
search booi.schot
nameserver 127.0.0.1
```

start windows 2003 server, enter the samba4 as DNS!

ping the domain, if it doesn't work, then add your redhats hostname and your realm to windows/system32/drivers/etc/hosts

join the windows computer to the domain

reboot the windows

log on with administrator stargate

start run dsa.msc to manage samba4

create an OU, a user and a GPO, test that it works

Part VII. selinux

Table of Contents

Chapter 19. introduction to SELinux

Security Enhanced Linux or **SELinux** is a set of modifications developed by the United States National Security Agency (NSA) to provide a variety of security policies for Linux. SELinux was released as open source at the end of 2000. Since kernel version 2.6 it is an integrated part of Linux.

SELinux offers security! SELinux can control what kind of access users have to files and processes. Even when a file received **chmod 777**, SELinux can still prevent applications from accessing it (Unix file permissions are checked first!). SELinux does this by placing users in **roles** that represent a security context. Administrators have very strict control on access permissions granted to roles.

SELinux is present in the latest versions of Red Hat Enterprise Linux, Debian, CentOS, Fedora, and many other distributions..

19.1. selinux modes

selinux knows three modes: enforcing, permissive and disabled. The **enforcing** mode will enforce policies, and may deny access based on **selinux rules**. The **permissive** mode will not enforce policies, but can still log actions that would have been denied in **enforcing** mode. The **disabled** mode disables **selinux**.

19.2. logging

Verify that **syslog** is running and activated on boot to enable logging of deny messages in **/var/log/messages**.

```
[root@rhel55 ~]# chkconfig --list syslog
syslog          0:off 1:off 2:on 3:on 4:on 5:on 6:off
```

Verify that **auditd** is running and activated on boot to enable logging of easier to read messages in **/var/log/audit/audit.log**.

```
[root@rhel55 ~]# chkconfig --list auditd
auditd          0:off 1:off 2:on 3:on 4:on 5:on 6:off
```

If not activated, then run **chkconfig --levels 2345 auditd on** and **service auditd start**.

```
[root@rhel55 ~]# service auditd status
auditd (pid  1660) is running...
[root@rhel55 ~]# service syslog status
syslogd (pid  1688) is running...
klogd (pid  1691) is running...
```

The **/var/log/messages** log file will tell you that **selinux** is disabled.

```
root@deb503:~# grep -i selinux /var/log/messages
Jun 25 15:59:34 deb503 kernel: [    0.084083] SELinux:  Disabled at boot.
```

Or that it is enabled.

```
root@deb503:~# grep SELinux /var/log/messages | grep -i Init
Jun 25 15:09:52 deb503 kernel: [    0.084094] SELinux:  Initializing.
```

19.3. activating selinux

On RHEL you can use the GUI tool to activate **selinux**, on Debian there is the **selinux-activate** command. Activation requires a reboot.

```
root@deb503:~# selinux-activate
Activating SE Linux
Searching for GRUB installation directory ... found: /boot/grub
Searching for default file ... found: /boot/grub/default
Testing for an existing GRUB menu.lst file ... found: /boot/grub/menu.lst
Searching for splash image ... none found, skipping ...
Found kernel: /boot/vmlinuz-2.6.26-2-686
Updating /boot/grub/menu.lst ... done

SE Linux is activated.  You may need to reboot now.
```

19.4. getenforce

Use **getenforce** to verify whether selinux is **enforced**, **disabled** or **permissive**.

```
[root@rhel55 ~]# getenforce
Permissive
```

The **/selinux/enforce** file contains 1 when enforcing, and 0 when permissive mode is active.

```
root@fedora13 ~# cat /selinux/enforce
1root@fedora13 ~#
```

19.5. setenforce

You can use **setenforce** to switch between the **Permissive** or the **Enforcing** state once **selinux** is activated..

```
[root@rhel55 ~]# setenforce Enforcing
[root@rhel55 ~]# getenforce
Enforcing
[root@rhel55 ~]# setenforce Permissive
[root@rhel55 ~]# qetenforce
Permissive
```

Or you could just use 0 and 1 as argument.

```
[root@centos65 ~]# setenforce 1
[root@centos65 ~]# getenforce
Enforcing
[root@centos65 ~]# setenforce 0
[root@centos65 ~]# getenforce
Permissive
[root@centos65 ~]#
```

19.6. sestatus

You can see the current **selinux** status and policy with the **sestatus** command.

```
[root@rhel55 ~]# sestatus
SELinux status:                 enabled
SELinuxfs mount:                /selinux
Current mode:                   permissive
Mode from config file:          permissive
Policy version:                 21
Policy from config file:        targeted
```

19.7. policy

Most Red Hat server will have the **targeted** policy. Only NSA/FBI/CIA/DOD/HLS use the **mls** policy.

The targted policy will protect hundreds of processes, but lets other processes run 'unconfined' (= they can do anything).

19.8. /etc/selinux/config

The main configuration file for **selinux** is **/etc/selinux/config**. When in **permissive** mode, the file looks like this.

The targeted policy is selected in **/etc/selinux/config**.

```
[root@centos65 ~]# cat /etc/selinux/config
# This file controls the state of SELinux on the system.
# SELINUX= can take one of these three values:
#       enforcing - SELinux security policy is enforced.
#       permissive - SELinux prints warnings instead of enforcing.
#       disabled - SELinux is fully disabled.
SELINUX=permissive
# SELINUXTYPE= type of policy in use. Possible values are:
#       targeted - Only targeted network daemons are protected.
#       strict - Full SELinux protection.
SELINUXTYPE=targeted
```

19.9. DAC or MAC

Standard Unix permissions use **Discretionary Access Control** to set permissions on files. This means that a user that owns a file, can make it world readable by typing **chmod 777 $file**.

With **selinux** the kernel will enforce **Mandatory Access Control** which strictly controls what processes or threads can do with files (superseding DAC). Processes are confined by the kernel to the minimum access they require.

SELinux MAC is about labeling and type enforcing! Files, processes, etc are all labeled with an SELinux context. For files, these are extended attributes, for processes this is managed by the kernel.

The format of the labels is as follows:

```
user:role:type:(level)
```

We only use the **type** label in the targeted policy.

19.10. ls -Z

To see the DAC permissions on a file, use **ls -l** to display user and group **owner** and permissions.

For MAC permissions there is new **-Z** option added to **ls**. The output shows that file in **/root** have a XXXtype of **admin_home_t**.

```
[root@centos65 ~]# ls -Z
-rw-------. root root system_u:object_r:admin_home_t:s0 anaconda-ks.cfg
-rw-r--r--. root root system_u:object_r:admin_home_t:s0 install.log
-rw-r--r--. root root system_u:object_r:admin_home_t:s0 install.log.syslog

[root@centos65 ~]# useradd -m -s /bin/bash pol
[root@centos65 ~]# ls -Z /home/pol/.bashrc
-rw-r--r--. pol pol unconfined_u:object_r:user_home_t:s0 /home/pol/.bashrc
```

19.11. -Z

There are also some other tools with the -Z switch:

```
mkdir -Z
cp -Z
ps -Z
netstat -Z
...
```

19.12. /selinux

When selinux is active, there is a new virtual file system named **/selinux**. (You can compare it to /proc and /dev.)

```
[root@centos65 ~]# ls -l /selinux/
total 0
-rw-rw-rw-.  1 root root     0 Apr 12 19:40 access
dr-xr-xr-x.  2 root root     0 Apr 12 19:40 avc
dr-xr-xr-x.  2 root root     0 Apr 12 19:40 booleans
-rw-r--r--.  1 root root     0 Apr 12 19:40 checkreqprot
dr-xr-xr-x. 83 root root     0 Apr 12 19:40 class
--w-------.  1 root root     0 Apr 12 19:40 commit_pending_bools
-rw-rw-rw-.  1 root root     0 Apr 12 19:40 context
-rw-rw-rw-.  1 root root     0 Apr 12 19:40 create
-r--r--r--.  1 root root     0 Apr 12 19:40 deny_unknown
--w-------.  1 root root     0 Apr 12 19:40 disable
-rw-r--r--.  1 root root     0 Apr 12 19:40 enforce
dr-xr-xr-x.  2 root root     0 Apr 12 19:40 initial_contexts
-rw-------.  1 root root     0 Apr 12 19:40 load
-rw-rw-rw-.  1 root root     0 Apr 12 19:40 member
-r--r--r--.  1 root root     0 Apr 12 19:40 mls
crw-rw-rw-.  1 root root 1, 3 Apr 12 19:40 null
-r--------.  1 root root     0 Apr 12 19:40 policy
dr-xr-xr-x.  2 root root     0 Apr 12 19:40 policy_capabilities
-r--r--r--.  1 root root     0 Apr 12 19:40 policyvers
-r--r--r--.  1 root root     0 Apr 12 19:40 reject_unknown
-rw-rw-rw-.  1 root root     0 Apr 12 19:40 relabel
-r--r--r--.  1 root root     0 Apr 12 19:40 status
-rw-rw-rw-.  1 root root     0 Apr 12 19:40 user
```

Although some files in **/selinux** appear wih size 0, they often contain a boolean value. Check **/selinux/enforce** to see if selinux is running in enforced mode.

```
[root@RHEL5 ~]# ls -l /selinux/enforce
-rw-r--r-- 1 root root 0 Apr 29 08:21 /selinux/enforce
[root@RHEL5 ~]# echo $(cat /selinux/enforce)
1
```

19.13. identity

The **SELinux Identity** of a user is distinct from the user ID. An identity is part of a security context, and (via domains) determines what you can do. The screenshot shows user **root** having identity **user_u**.

```
[root@rhel55 ~]# id -Z
user_u:system_r:unconfined_t
```

19.14. role

The **selinux role** defines the domains that can be used. A **role** is denied to enter a domain, unless the **role** is explicitly authorized to do so.

19.15. type (or domain)

The **selinux context** is the security context of a process. An **selinux type** determines what a process can do. The screenshot shows init running in type **init_t** and the mingetty's running in type **getty_t**.

```
[root@centos65 ~]# ps fax -Z | grep /sbin/init
system_u:system_r:init_t:s0          1 ?           Ss      0:00 /sbin/init
[root@centos65 ~]# ps fax -Z | grep getty_t
system_u:system_r:getty_t:s0      1307 tty1    Ss+   0:00 /sbin/mingetty /dev/tty1
system_u:system_r:getty_t:s0      1309 tty2    Ss+   0:00 /sbin/mingetty /dev/tty2
system_u:system_r:getty_t:s0      1311 tty3    Ss+   0:00 /sbin/mingetty /dev/tty3
system_u:system_r:getty_t:s0      1313 tty4    Ss+   0:00 /sbin/mingetty /dev/tty4
system_u:system_r:getty_t:s0      1320 tty5    Ss+   0:00 /sbin/mingetty /dev/tty5
system_u:system_r:getty_t:s0      1322 tty6    Ss+   0:00 /sbin/mingetty /dev/tty6
```

The **selinux type** is similar to an **selinux domain**, but refers to directories and files instead of processes.

Hundreds of binaries also have a type:

```
[root@centos65 sbin]# ls -lZ useradd usermod userdel httpd postcat postfix
-rwxr-xr-x. root root system_u:object_r:httpd_exec_t:s0 httpd
-rwxr-xr-x. root root system_u:object_r:postfix_master_exec_t:s0 postcat
-rwxr-xr-x. root root system_u:object_r:postfix_master_exec_t:s0 postfix
-rwxr-x---. root root system_u:object_r:useradd_exec_t:s0 useradd
-rwxr-x---. root root system_u:object_r:useradd_exec_t:s0 userdel
-rwxr-x---. root root system_u:object_r:useradd_exec_t:s0 usermod
```

Ports also have a context.

```
[root@centos65 sbin]# netstat -nptlZ | tr -s ' ' | cut -d' ' -f6-

Foreign Address State PID/Program name Security Context
LISTEN 1096/rpcbind system_u:system_r:rpcbind_t:s0
LISTEN 1208/sshd system_u:system_r:sshd_t:s0-s0:c0.c1023
LISTEN 1284/master system_u:system_r:postfix_master_t:s0
LISTEN 1114/rpc.statd system_u:system_r:rpcd_t:s0
LISTEN 1096/rpcbind system_u:system_r:rpcbind_t:s0
LISTEN 1666/httpd unconfined_u:system_r:httpd_t:s0
LISTEN 1208/sshd system_u:system_r:sshd_t:s0-s0:c0.c1023
LISTEN 1114/rpc.statd system_u:system_r:rpcd_t:s0
LISTEN 1284/master system_u:system_r:postfix_master_t:s0
```

You can also get a list of ports that are managed by SELinux:

```
[root@centos65 ~]# semanage port -l | tail
xfs_port_t                      tcp     7100
xserver_port_t                  tcp     6000-6150
zabbix_agent_port_t             tcp     10050
zabbix_port_t                   tcp     10051
zarafa_port_t                   tcp     236, 237
zebra_port_t                    tcp     2600-2604, 2606
zebra_port_t                    udp     2600-2604, 2606
zented_port_t                   tcp     1229
zented_port_t                   udp     1229
zope_port_t                     tcp     8021
```

19.16. security context

The combination of identity, role and domain or type make up the **selinux security context**. The **id** will show you your security context in the form identity:role:domain.

```
[paul@RHEL5 ~]$ id | cut -d' ' -f4
context=user_u:system_r:unconfined_t
```

The **ls -Z** command shows the security context for a file in the form identity:role:type.

```
[paul@RHEL5 ~]$ ls -Z test
-rw-rw-r--   paul paul user_u:object_r:user_home_t        test
```

The security context for processes visible in /proc defines both the type (of the file in /proc) and the domain (of the running process). Let's take a look at the init process and /proc/1/ .

The init process runs in domain **init_t**.

```
[root@RHEL5 ~]# ps -ZC init
LABEL                            PID TTY          TIME CMD
system_u:system_r:init_t          1 ?        00:00:01 init
```

The **/proc/1/** directory, which identifies the **init** process, has type **init_t**.

```
[root@RHEL5 ~]# ls -Zd /proc/1/
dr-xr-xr-x  root root system_u:system_r:init_t          /proc/1/
```

It is not a coincidence that the domain of the **init** process and the type of **/proc/1/** are both **init_t**.

Don't try to use **chcon** on /proc! It will not work.

19.17. transition

An **selinux transition** (aka an selinux labelling) determines the security context that will be assigned. A transition of process domains is used when you execute a process. A transition of file type happens when you create a file.

An example of file type transition.

```
[pol@centos65 ~]$ touch test /tmp/test
[pol@centos65 ~]$ ls -Z test
-rw-rw-r--. pol pol unconfined_u:object_r:user_home_t:s0 test
[pol@centos65 ~]$ ls -Z /tmp/test
-rw-rw-r--. pol pol unconfined_u:object_r:user_tmp_t:s0 /tmp/test
```

19.18. extended attributes

Extended attributes are used by **selinux** to store security contexts. These attributes can be viewed with **ls** when **selinux** is running.

```
[root@RHEL5 home]# ls --context
drwx------    paul paul system_u:object_r:user_home_dir_t paul
drwxr-xr-x    root root user_u:object_r:user_home_dir_t  project42
drwxr-xr-x    root root user_u:object_r:user_home_dir_t  project55
[root@RHEL5 home]# ls -Z
drwx------    paul paul system_u:object_r:user_home_dir_t paul
drwxr-xr-x    root root user_u:object_r:user_home_dir_t  project42
drwxr-xr-x    root root user_u:object_r:user_home_dir_t  project55
[root@RHEL5 home]#
```

When selinux is not running, then **getfattr** is the tool to use.

```
[root@RHEL5 etc]# getfattr -m . -d hosts
# file: hosts
security.selinux="system_u:object_r:etc_t:s0\000"
```

19.19. process security context

A new option is added to **ps** to see the selinux security context of processes.

```
[root@RHEL5 etc]# ps -ZC mingetty
LABEL                           PID TTY          TIME CMD
system_u:system_r:getty_t      2941 tty1     00:00:00 mingetty
system_u:system_r:getty_t      2942 tty2     00:00:00 mingetty
```

19.20. chcon

Use **chcon** to change the selinux security context.

This example shows how to use **chcon** to change the **type** of a file.

```
[root@rhel55 ~]# ls -Z /var/www/html/test42.txt
-rw-r--r--  root root user_u:object_r:httpd_sys_content_t /var/www/html/test4\
2.txt
[root@rhel55 ~]# chcon -t samba_share_t /var/www/html/test42.txt
[root@rhel55 ~]# ls -Z /var/www/html/test42.txt
-rw-r--r--  root root user_u:object_r:samba_share_t    /var/www/html/test42.txt
```

Be sure to read **man chcon**.

19.21. an example

The **Apache2 webserver** is by default targeted with **SELinux**. The next screenshot shows that any file created in **/var/www/html** will by default get the **httpd_sys_content_t** type.

```
[root@centos65 ~]# touch /var/www/html/test42.txt
[root@centos65 ~]# ls -Z /var/www/html/test42.txt
-rw-r--r--. root root unconfined_u:object_r:httpd_sys_content_t:s0 /var/www/h\
tml/test42.txt
```

Files created elsewhere do not get this type.

```
[root@centos65 ~]# touch /root/test42.txt
[root@centos65 ~]# ls -Z /root/test42.txt
-rw-r--r--. root root unconfined_u:object_r:admin_home_t:s0 /root/test42.txt
```

Make sure **Apache2** runs.

```
[root@centos65 ~]# service httpd restart
Stopping httpd:                                          [  OK  ]
Starting httpd:                                          [  OK  ]
```

Will this work ? Yes it does.

```
[root@centos65 ~]# wget http://localhost/test42.txt
--2014-04-12 20:56:47--  http://localhost/test42.txt
Resolving localhost... ::1, 127.0.0.1
Connecting to localhost|::1|:80... connected.
HTTP request sent, awaiting response... 200 OK
Length: 0 [text/plain]
Saving to: "test42.txt"
...
```

Why does this work ? Because Apache2 runs in the **httpd_t** domain and the files in **/var/www/html** have the **httpd_sys_content_t** type.

```
[root@centos65 ~]# ps -ZC httpd | head -4
LABEL                           PID TTY        TIME CMD
unconfined_u:system_r:httpd_t:s0 1666 ?      00:00:00 httpd
unconfined_u:system_r:httpd_t:s0 1668 ?      00:00:00 httpd
unconfined_u:system_r:httpd_t:s0 1669 ?      00:00:00 httpd
```

So let's set SELinux to **enforcing** and change the **type** of this file.

```
[root@centos65 ~]# chcon -t samba_share_t /var/www/html/test42.txt
[root@centos65 ~]# ls -Z /var/www/html/test42.txt
-rw-r--r--. root root unconfined_u:object_r:samba_share_t:s0 /var/www/html/t\
est42.txt
[root@centos65 ~]# setenforce 1
[root@centos65 ~]# getenforce
Enforcing
```

There are two possibilities now: either it works, or it fails. It works when **selinux** is in **permissive mode**, it fails when in **enforcing mode**.

```
[root@centos65 ~]# wget http://localhost/test42.txt
--2014-04-12 21:05:02--  http://localhost/test42.txt
Resolving localhost... ::1, 127.0.0.1
Connecting to localhost|::1|:80... connected.
HTTP request sent, awaiting response... 403 Forbidden
2014-04-12 21:05:02 ERROR 403: Forbidden.
```

The log file gives you a cryptic message...

```
[root@centos65 ~]# tail -3 /var/log/audit/audit.log
type=SYSCALL msg=audit(1398200702.803:64): arch=c000003e syscall=4 succ\
ess=no exit=-13 a0=7f5fbc334d70 a1=7fff553b4f10 a2=7fff553b4f10 a3=0 it\
ems=0 ppid=1666 pid=1673 auid=500 uid=48 gid=48 euid=48 suid=48 fsuid=4\
8 egid=48 sgid=48 fsgid=48 tty=(none) ses=1 comm="httpd" exe="/usr/sbin\
/httpd" subj=unconfined_u:system_r:httpd_t:s0 key=(null)
type=AVC msg=audit(1398200702.804:65): avc:  denied  { getattr } for  p\
id=1673 comm="httpd" path="/var/www/html/test42.txt" dev=dm-0 ino=26324\
1 scontext=unconfined_u:system_r:httpd_t:s0 tcontext=unconfined_u:objec\
t_r:samba_share_t:s0 tclass=file
type=SYSCALL msg=audit(1398200702.804:65): arch=c000003e syscall=6 succ\
ess=no exit=-13 a0=7f5fbc334e40 a1=7fff553b4f10 a2=7fff553b4f10 a3=1 it\
ems=0 ppid=1666 pid=1673 auid=500 uid=48 gid=48 euid=48 suid=48 fsuid=4\
8 egid=48 sgid=48 fsgid=48 tty=(none) ses=1 comm="httpd" exe="/usr/sbin\
/httpd" subj=unconfined_u:system_r:httpd_t:s0 key=(null)
```

And **/var/log/messages** mentions nothing of the failed download.

19.22. setroubleshoot

The log file above was not very helpful, but these two packages can make your life much easier.

```
[root@centos65 ~]# yum -y install setroubleshoot setroubleshoot-server
```

You need to **reboot** for this to work...

So we reboot, restart the httpd server, reactive SELinux Enforce, and do the wget again... and it fails (because of SELinux).

```
[root@centos65 ~]# service httpd restart
Stopping httpd:                                         [FAILED]
Starting httpd:                                         [ OK ]
[root@centos65 ~]# getenforce
Permissive
[root@centos65 ~]# setenforce  1
[root@centos65 ~]# getenforce
Enforcing
[root@centos65 ~]# wget http://localhost/test42.txt
--2014-04-12 21:44:13--  http://localhost/test42.txt
Resolving localhost... ::1, 127.0.0.1
Connecting to localhost|::1|:80... connected.
HTTP request sent, awaiting response... 403 Forbidden
2014-04-12 21:44:13 ERROR 403: Forbidden.
```

The **/var/log/audit/** is still not out best friend, but take a look at **/var/log/messages**.

```
[root@centos65 ~]# tail -2 /var/log/messages
Apr 12 21:44:16  centos65  setroubleshoot: SELinux is preventing /usr/sbin/h\
ttpd from getattr access on the file /var/www/html/test42.txt. For complete \
SELinux messages. run sealert -l b2a84386-54c1-4344-96fb-dcf969776696
Apr 12 21:44:16  centos65  setroubleshoot: SELinux is preventing /usr/sbin/h\
ttpd from getattr access on the file /var/www/html/test42.txt. For complete \
SELinux messages. run sealert -l b2a84386-54c1-4344-96fb-dcf969776696
```

So we run the command it suggests...

```
[root@centos65 ~]# sealert -l b2a84386-54c1-4344-96fb-dcf969776696
SELinux is preventing /usr/sbin/httpd from getattr access on the file /va\
r/www/html/test42.txt.

*****  Plugin restorecon (92.2 confidence) suggests  ********************

If you want to fix the label.
/var/www/html/test42.txt default label should be httpd_sys_content_t.
Then you can run restorecon.
Do
# /sbin/restorecon -v /var/www/html/test42.txt
...
```

We follow the friendly advice and try again to download our file:

```
[root@centos65 ~]# /sbin/restorecon -v /var/www/html/test42.txt
/sbin/restorecon reset /var/www/html/test42.txt context unconfined_u:objec\
t_r:samba_share_t:s0->unconfined_u:object_r:httpd_sys_content_t:s0
[root@centos65 ~]# wget http://localhost/test42.txt
--2014-04-12 21:54:03--  http://localhost/test42.txt
Resolving localhost... ::1, 127.0.0.1
Connecting to localhost|::1|:80... connected.
HTTP request sent, awaiting response... 200 OK
```

It works!

19.23. booleans

Booleans are on/off switches

```
[root@centos65 ~]# getsebool -a | head
abrt_anon_write --> off
abrt_handle_event --> off
allow_console_login --> on
allow_cvs_read_shadow --> off
allow_daemons_dump_core --> on
allow_daemons_use_tcp_wrapper --> off
allow_daemons_use_tty --> on
allow_domain_fd_use --> on
allow_execheap --> off
allow_execmem --> on
```

You can set and read individual booleans.

```
[root@centos65 ~]# setsebool httpd_read_user_content=1
[root@centos65 ~]# getsebool httpd_read_user_content
httpd_read_user_content --> on
[root@centos65 ~]# setsebool httpd_enable_homedirs=1
[root@centos65 ~]# getsebool httpd_enable_homedirs
httpd_enable_homedirs --> on
```

You can set these booleans permanent.

```
[root@centos65 ~]# setsebool -P httpd_enable_homedirs=1
[root@centos65 ~]# setsebool -P httpd_read_user_content=1
```

The above commands regenerate the complete /etc/selinux/targeted directory!

```
[root@centos65 ~]# cat /etc/selinux/targeted/modules/active/booleans.local
# This file is auto-generated by libsemanage
# Do not edit directly.

httpd_enable_homedirs=1
httpd_read_user_content=1
```

Part VIII. introducing git

Table of Contents

Chapter 20. git

This chapter is an introduction to using **git** on the command line. The **git repository** is hosted by **github**, but you are free to choose another server (or create your own).

There are many excellent online tutorials for **git**. This list can save you one Google query:

```
http://gitimmersion.com/
http://git-scm.com/book
```

20.1. git

Linus Torvalds created **git** back in 2005 when Bitkeeper changed its license and the Linux kernel developers where no longer able to use it for free.

git quickly became popular and is now the most widely used **distributed version control** system in the world.

Geek and Poke demonstrates why we need version control (image property of Geek and Poke CCA 3.0).

Besides **source code** for software, you can also find German and Icelandic **law** on github (and probably much more by the time you are reading this).

20.2. installing git

We install **git** with **aptitude install git** as seen in this screenshot on Debian 6.

```
root@debian6:~# aptitude install git
The following NEW packages will be installed:
  git libcurl3-gnutls{a} liberror-perl{a}
0 packages upgraded, 3 newly installed, 0 to remove and 0 not upgraded.
...
Processing triggers for man-db ...
Setting up libcurl3-gnutls (7.21.0-2.1+squeeze2) ...
Setting up liberror-perl (0.17-1) ...
Setting up git (1:1.7.2.5-3) ...
```

20.3. starting a project

First we create a project directory, with a simple file in it.

```
paul@debian6~$ mkdir project42
paul@debian6~$ cd project42/
paul@debian6~/project42$ echo "echo The answer is 42." >> question.sh
```

20.3.1. git init

Then we tell **git** to create an empty git repository in this directory.

```
paul@debian6~/project42$ ls -la
total 12
drwxrwxr-x  2 paul paul 4096 Dec  8 16:41 .
drwxr-xr-x 46 paul paul 4096 Dec  8 16:41 ..
-rw-rw-r--  1 paul paul   23 Dec  8 16:41 question.sh
paul@debian6~/project42$ git init
Initialized empty Git repository in /home/paul/project42/.git/
paul@debian6~/project42$ ls -la
total 16
drwxrwxr-x  3 paul paul 4096 Dec  8 16:44 .
drwxr-xr-x 46 paul paul 4096 Dec  8 16:41 ..
drwxrwxr-x  7 paul paul 4096 Dec  8 16:44 .git
-rw-rw-r--  1 paul paul   23 Dec  8 16:41 question.sh
```

20.3.2. git config

Next we use **git config** to set some global options.

```
paul@debian6$ git config --global user.name Paul
paul@debian6$ git config --global user.email "paul.cobbaut@gmail.com"
paul@debian6$ git config --global core.editor vi
```

We can verify this config in ~/.**gitconfig**:

```
paul@debian6~/project42$ cat ~/.gitconfig
[user]
 name = Paul
 email = paul.cobbaut@gmail.com
[core]
 editor = vi
```

20.3.3. git add

Time now to add file to our project with **git add**, and verify that it is added with **git status**.

```
paul@debian6~/project42$ git add question.sh
paul@debian6~/project42$ git status
# On branch master
#
# Initial commit
#
# Changes to be committed:
#   (use "git rm --cached <file>..." to unstage)
#
# new file:   question.sh
#
```

The **git status** tells us there is a new file ready to be committed.

20.3.4. git commit

With **git commit** you force git to record all added files (and all changes to those files) permanently.

```
paul@debian6~/project42$ git commit -m "starting a project"
[master (root-commit) 5c10768] starting a project
 1 file changed, 1 insertion(+)
 create mode 100644 question.sh
paul@debian6~/project42$ git status
# On branch master
nothing to commit (working directory clean)
```

20.3.5. changing a committed file

The screenshots below show several steps. First we change a file:

```
paul@debian6~/project42$ git status
# On branch master
nothing to commit (working directory clean)
paul@debian6~/project42$ vi question.sh
```

Then we verify the status and see that it is modified:

```
paul@debian6~/project42$ git status
# On branch master
# Changes not staged for commit:
#   (use "git add <file>..." to update what will be committed)
#   (use "git checkout -- <file>..." to discard changes in working directory)
#
# modified:   question.sh
#
no changes added to commit (use "git add" and/or "git commit -a")
```

Next we add it to the git repository.

```
paul@debian6~/project42$ git add question.sh
paul@debian6~/project42$ git commit -m "adding a she-bang to the main script"
[master 86b8347] adding a she-bang to the main script
 1 file changed, 1 insertion(+)
paul@debian6~/project42$ git status
# On branch master
nothing to commit (working directory clean)
```

20.3.6. git log

We can see all our commits again using **git log**.

```
paul@debian6~/project42$ git log
commit 86b8347192ea025815df7a8e628d99474b41fb6c
Author: Paul <paul.cobbaut@gmail.com>
Date:   Sat Dec 8 17:12:24 2012 +0100

    adding a she-bang to the main script

commit 5c10768f29aecc16161fb197765e0f14383f7bca
Author: Paul <paul.cobbaut@gmail.com>
Date:   Sat Dec 8 17:09:29 2012 +0100

    starting a project
```

The log format can be changed.

```
paul@debian6~/project42$ git log --pretty=oneline
86b8347192ea025815df7a8e628d99474b41fb6c adding a she-bang to the main script
5c10768f29aecc16161fb197765e0f14383f7bca starting a project
```

The log format can be customized a lot.

```
paul@debian6~/project42$ git log --pretty=format:"%an: %ar :%s"
Paul: 8 minutes ago :adding a she-bang to the main script
Paul: 11 minutes ago :starting a project
```

20.3.7. git mv

Renaming a file can be done with **mv** followed by a **git remove** and a **git add** of the new filename. But it can be done easier and in one command using **git mv**.

```
paul@debian6~/project42$ git mv question.sh thequestion.sh
paul@debian6~/project42$ git status
# On branch master
# Changes to be committed:
#   (use "git reset HEAD <file>..." to unstage)
#
# renamed:    question.sh -> thequestion.sh
#
paul@debian6~/project42$ git commit -m "improved naming scheme"
[master 69b2c8b] improved naming scheme
 1 file changed, 0 insertions(+), 0 deletions(-)
 rename question.sh => thequestion.sh (100%)
```

20.4. git branches

Working on the project can be done in one or more **git branches**. Here we create a new branch that will make changes to the script. We will **merge** this branch with the **master branch** when we are sure the script works. (It can be useful to add **git status** commands when practicing).

```
paul@debian6~/project42$ git branch
* master
paul@debian6~/project42$ git checkout -b newheader
Switched to a new branch 'newheader'
paul@debian6~/project42$ vi thequestion.sh
paul@debian6~/project42$ git add thequestion.sh
paul@debian6~/project42$ source thequestion.sh
The answer is 42.
```

It seems to work, so we commit in this branch.

```
paul@debian6~/project42$ git commit -m "adding a new company header"
[newheader 730a22b] adding a new company header
 1 file changed, 4 insertions(+)
paul@debian6~/project42$ git branch
  master
* newheader
paul@debian6~/project42$ cat thequestion.sh
#!/bin/bash
#
# copyright linux-training.be
#

echo The answer is 42.
```

Let us go back to the master branch and see what happened there.

```
paul@debian6~/project42$ git checkout master
Switched to branch 'master'
paul@debian6~/project42$ cat thequestion.sh
#!/bin/bash
echo The answer is 42.
```

Nothing happened in the master branch, because we worked in another branch.

When we are sure the branch is ready for production, then we merge it into the master branch.

```
paul@debian6~/project42$ cat thequestion.sh
#!/bin/bash
echo The answer is 42.
paul@debian6~/project42$ git merge newheader
Updating 69b2c8b..730a22b
Fast-forward
 thequestion.sh |    4 ++++
 1 file changed, 4 insertions(+)
paul@debian6~/project42$ cat thequestion.sh
#!/bin/bash
#
# copyright linux-training.be
#

echo The answer is 42.
```

The newheader branch can now be deleted.

```
paul@debian6~/project42$ git branch
* master
  newheader
paul@debian6~/project42$ git branch -d newheader
Deleted branch newheader (was 730a22b).
paul@debian6~/project42$ git branch
* master
```

20.5. to be continued...

The **git** story is not finished.

There are many excellent online tutorials for **git**. This list can save you one Google query:

```
http://gitimmersion.com/
http://git-scm.com/book
```

20.6. github.com

Create an account on **github.com**. This website is a frontend for an immense git server with over two and a half million users and almost five million projects (including Fedora, Linux kernel, Android, Ruby on Rails, Wine, X.org, VLC...)

```
https://github.com/signup/free
```

This account is free of charge, we will use it in the examples below.

20.7. add your public key to github

I prefer to use github with a **public key**, so it probably is a good idea that you also upload your public key to github.com.

You can upload your own key via the web interface:

```
https://github.com/settings/ssh
```

Please do not forget to protect your **private key**!

20.8. practice: git

1. Create a project on github to host a script that you wrote. Have at least two other people improve the script.

Part IX. ipv6

Table of Contents

Chapter 21. Introduction to ipv6

21.1. about ipv6

The **ipv6** protocol is designed to replace **ipv4**. Where **ip version 4** supports a maximum of four billion unique addresses, **ip version 6** expands this to **four billion times four billion times four billion times four billion** unique addresses. This is more than 100.000.000.000.000.000.000 ipv6 addresses per square cm on our planet. That should be enough, even if every cell phone, every coffee machine and every pair of socks gets an address.

Technically speaking ipv6 uses 128-bit addresses (instead of the 32-bit from ipv4). 128-bit addresses are **huge** numbers. In decimal it would amount up to 39 digits, in hexadecimal it looks like this:

```
fe80:0000:0000:0000:0a00:27ff:fe8e:8aa8
```

Luckily ipv6 allows us to omit leading zeroes. Our address from above then becomes:

```
fe80:0:0:0:a00:27ff:fe8e:8aa8
```

When a 16-bit block is zero, it can be written as **::**. Consecutive 16-bit blocks that are zero can also be written as **::**. So our address can from above can be shortened to:

```
fe80::a00:27ff:fe8e:8aa8
```

This **::** can only occur once! The following is not a valid ipv6 address:

```
fe80::20:2e4f::39ac
```

The ipv6 **localhost** address is **0000:0000:0000:0000:0000:0000:0000:0001**, which can be abbreviated to **::1**.

```
paul@debian5:~/github/lt/images$ /sbin/ifconfig lo | grep inet6
          inet6 addr: ::1/128 Scope:Host
```

21.2. network id and host id

One of the few similarities between ipv4 and ipv6 is that addresses have a host part and a network part determined by a subnet mask. Using the **cidr** notation this looks like this:

```
fe80::a00:27ff:fe8e:8aa8/64
```

The above address has 64 bits for the host id, theoretically allowing for 4 billion times four billion hosts.

The localhost address looks like this with cidr:

```
::1/128
```

21.3. host part generation

The host part of an automatically generated (stateless) ipv6 address contains part of the hosts mac address:

```
paul@debian5:~$ /sbin/ifconfig | head -3
```

```
eth3       Link encap:Ethernet  HWaddr 08:00:27:ab:67:30
           inet addr:192.168.1.29  Bcast:192.168.1.255  Mask:255.255.255.0
           inet6 addr: fe80::a00:27ff:feab:6730/64 Scope:Link
```

Some people are concerned about privacy here...

21.4. ipv4 mapped ipv6 address

Some applications use ipv4 addresses embedded in an ipv6 address. (Yes there will be an era of migration with both ipv4 and ipv6 in use.) The ipv6 address then looks like this:

```
::ffff:192.168.1.42/96
```

Indeed a mix of decimal and hexadecimal characters...

21.5. link local addresses

ipv6 addresses starting with **fe8.** can only be used on the local segment (replace the dot with an hexadecimal digit). This is the reason you see **Scope:Link** behind the address in this screenshot. This address serves only the **local link**.

```
paul@deb503:~$ /sbin/ifconfig | grep inet6
   inet6 addr: fe80::a00:27ff:fe8e:8aa8/64 Scope:Link
   inet6 addr: ::1/128 Scope:Host
```

These **link local** addresses all begin with **fe8.**.

Every ipv6 enabled nic will get an address in this range.

21.6. unique local addresses

The now obsolete system of **site local addresses** similar to ipv4 private ranges is replaced with a system of globally unique local ipv6 addresses. This to prevent duplicates when joining of networks within **site local** ranges.

All **unique local** addresses strat with **fd...**

21.7. globally unique unicast addresses

Since **ipv6** was designed to have multiple ip addresses per interface, the **global ipv6 address** can be used next to the **link local address**.

These **globally unique** addresses all begin with **2...** or **3...** as the first 16-bits.

21.8. 6to4

6to4 is defined in rfc's 2893 and 3056 as one possible way to transition between ipv4 and ipv6 by creating an ipv6 tunnel.

It encodes an ipv4 address in an ipv6 address that starts with **2002**. For example 192.168.1.42/24 will be encoded as:

```
2002:c0a8:12a:18::1
```

You can use the command below to convert any ipv4 address to this range.

```
paul@ubu1010:~$ printf "2002:%02x%02x:%02x%02x:%04x::1\n" `echo 192.168.1.42/24 \
|tr "./" " "`
2002:c0a8:012a:0018::1
```

21.9. ISP

Should you be so lucky to get an ipv6 address from an **isp**, then it will start with **2001:**.

21.10. non routable addresses

Comparable to **example.com** for DNS, the following ipv6 address ranges are reserved for examples, and not routable on the internet.

```
3fff:ffff::/32
2001:0db8::/32
```

21.11. ping6

Use **ping6** to test connectivity between ipv6 hosts. You need to specify the interface (there is no routing table for 'random' generated ipv6 link local addresses).

```
[root@fedora14 ~]# ping6 -I eth0 fe80::a00:27ff:fecd:7ffc
PING fe80::a00:27ff:fecd:7ffc(fe80::a00:27ff:fecd:7ffc) from fe80::a00:27ff:fe3c:4346 eth0: 56
64 bytes from fe80::a00:27ff:fecd:7ffc: icmp_seq=1 ttl=64 time=0.586 ms
64 bytes from fe80::a00:27ff:fecd:7ffc: icmp_seq=2 ttl=64 time=3.95 ms
64 bytes from fe80::a00:27ff:fecd:7ffc: icmp_seq=3 ttl=64 time=1.53 ms
```

Below a multicast ping6 that recieves replies from three ip6 hosts on the same network.

```
[root@fedora14 ~]# ping6 -I eth0 ff02::1
PING ff02::1(ff02::1) from fe80::a00:27ff:fe3c:4346 eth0: 56 data bytes
64 bytes from fe80::a00:27ff:fe3c:4346: icmp_seq=1 ttl=64 time=0.598 ms
64 bytes from fe80::a00:27ff:fecd:7ffc: icmp_seq=1 ttl=64 time=1.87 ms (DUP!)
64 bytes from fe80::8e7b:9dff:fed6:dff2: icmp_seq=1 ttl=64 time=535 ms (DUP!)
64 bytes from fe80::a00:27ff:fe3c:4346: icmp_seq=2 ttl=64 time=0.106 ms
64 bytes from fe80::8e7b:9dff:fed6:dff2: icmp_seq=2 ttl=64 time=1.79 ms (DUP!)
64 bytes from fe80::a00:27ff:fecd:7ffc: icmp_seq=2 ttl=64 time=2.48 ms (DUP!)
```

21.12. Belgium and ipv6

A lot of information on ipv6 in Belgium can be found at www.ipv6council.be.

Sites like ipv6.belgium.be, www.bipt.be and www.bricozone.be are enabled for ipv6. Some Universities also: fundp.ac.be (Namur) and ulg.ac.be (Liege).

21.13. other websites

Other useful websites for testing ipv6 are:

```
test-ipv6.com
ipv6-test.com
```

Going to the ipv6-test.com website will test whether you have a valid accessible ipv6 address.

Your internet connection is **IPv6** capable

2002:51a5:657d::1

Telenet

Address type is

6to4

6to4 mapping to IPv4 address **81.165.101.125**

Your internet connection is IPv4 capable

81.165.101.125

d51A5657D.access.telenet.be

Going to the test-ipv6.com website will also test whether you have a valid accessible ipv6 address.

Test your IPv6 connectivity.

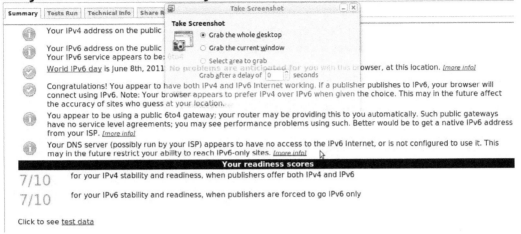

Summary	Tests Run	Technical Info	Share R

Your IPv4 address on the public

Your IPv6 address on the public
Your IPv6 service appears to be: 6to4

World IPv6 day is June 8th, 2011. No problems are anticipated for you with this browser, at this location. *[more info]*

Congratulations! You appear to have both IPv4 and IPv6 Internet working. If a publisher publishes to IPv6, your browser will connect using IPv6. Note: Your browser appears to prefer IPv4 over IPv6 when given the choice. This may in the future affect the accuracy of sites who guess at your location.

You appear to be using a public 6to4 gateway; your router may be providing this to you automatically. Such public gateways have no service level agreements; you may see performance problems using such. Better would be to get a native IPv6 address from your ISP. *[more info]*

Your DNS server (possibly run by your ISP) appears to have no access to the IPv6 Internet, or is not configured to use it. This may in the future restrict your ability to reach IPv6-only sites. *[more info]*

Your readiness scores

7/10   for your IPv4 stability and readiness, when publishers offer both IPv4 and IPv6

7/10   for your IPv6 stability and readiness, when publishers are forced to go IPv6 only

Click to see test data

21.14. 6to4 gateways

To access ipv4 only websites when on ipv6 you can use sixxs.net (more specifically http://www.sixxs.net/tools/gateway/) as a gatway.

For example use http://www.slashdot.org.sixxs.org/ instead of http://slashdot.org

21.15. ping6 and dns

Below a screenshot of a **ping6** from behind a 6to4 connection.

```
81.165.101.125        195.130.131.4          DNS      Standard query AAAA ipv6-test.com
195.130.131.4         81.165.101.125         DNS      Standard query response AAAA 2001:41d0:2:67d1::7e57:1
2002:51a5:657d::1     2001:41d0:2:67d1::7e57:1 ICMPv6  Echo request
2001:41d0:2:67d1::7e57:1 2002:51a5:657d::1   ICMPv6   Echo reply
2002:51a5:657d::1     2001:41d0:2:67d1::7e57:1 ICMPv6  Echo request
2001:41d0:2:67d1::7e57:1 2002:51a5:657d::1   ICMPv6   Echo reply
```

21.16. ipv6 and tcp/http

Below a screenshot of a tcp handshake and http connection over ipv6.

Source	Destination	Protocol	Info
2002:51a5:657d::1	2001:41d0:2:67d1::7e57:1	TCP	38036 > http [SYN] Seq=0 Win=5648 L
2001:41d0:2:67d1::7e57:1	2002:51a5:657d::1	TCP	http > 38036 [SYN, ACK] Seq=0 Ack=1
2002:51a5:657d::1	2001:41d0:2:67d1::7e57:1	TCP	38036 > http [ACK] Seq=1 Ack=1 Win=
2002:51a5:657d::1	2001:41d0:2:67d1::7e57:1	HTTP	GET /json/addrinfo.php?PHPSESSID=19
2001:41d0:2:67d1::7e57:1	2002:51a5:657d::1	TCP	http > 38036 [ACK] Seq=1 Ack=708 Wi
2001:41d0:2:67d1::7e57:1	2002:51a5:657d::1	HTTP	HTTP/1.1 200 OK (text/javascript)

21.17. ipv6 PTR record

As seen in the DNS chapter, ipv6 PTR records are in the ip6.net domain, and have 32 generations of child domains.

```
▷ Frame 46 (132 bytes on wire, 132 bytes captured)
▷ Ethernet II, Src: Apple_5d:2e:52 (00:26:bb:5d:2e:52), Dst: Riverdel_cf:6a:10 (00:30:b8:cf:6a:10)
▷ Internet Protocol, Src: 81.165.101.125 (81.165.101.125), Dst: 195.130.131.4 (195.130.131.4)
▷ User Datagram Protocol, Src Port: 34361 (34361), Dst Port: domain (53)
▽ Domain Name System (query)
     [Response In: 47]
     Transaction ID: 0xcfe3
  ▷ Flags: 0x0100 (Standard query)
     Questions: 1
     Answer RRs: 0
     Authority RRs: 0
     Additional RRs: 0
  ▽ Queries
     ▷ 1.0.0.0.7.5.e.7.0.0.0.0.0.0.0.0.1.d.7.6.2.0.0.0.0.d.1.4.1.0.0.2.ip6.arpa: type PTR, class IN
```

21.18. 6to4 setup on Linux

Below a transcript of a 6to4 setup on Linux.

Thanks to http://www.anyweb.co.nz/tutorial/v6Linux6to4 and http://mirrors.bieringer.de/Linux+IPv6-HOWTO/ and tldp.org!

```
root@mac:~# ifconfig
eth0      Link encap:Ethernet  HWaddr 00:26:bb:5d:2e:52
          inet addr:81.165.101.125  Bcast:255.255.255.255  Mask:255.255.248.0
```

```
                    inet6 addr: fe80::226:bbff:fe5d:2e52/64 Scope:Link
                    UP BROADCAST RUNNING MULTICAST  MTU:1500  Metric:1
                    RX packets:5926044 errors:0 dropped:0 overruns:0 frame:0
                    TX packets:2985892 errors:0 dropped:0 overruns:0 carrier:0
                    collisions:0 txqueuelen:1000
                    RX bytes:4274849823 (4.2 GB)  TX bytes:237002019 (237.0 MB)
                    Interrupt:43 Base address:0x8000

lo          Link encap:Local Loopback
            inet addr:127.0.0.1  Mask:255.0.0.0
            inet6 addr: ::1/128 Scope:Host
            UP LOOPBACK RUNNING  MTU:16436  Metric:1
            RX packets:598 errors:0 dropped:0 overruns:0 frame:0
            TX packets:598 errors:0 dropped:0 overruns:0 carrier:0
            collisions:0 txqueuelen:0
            RX bytes:61737 (61.7 KB)  TX bytes:61737 (61.7 KB)

root@mac:~# sysctl -w net.ipv6.conf.default.forwarding=1
net.ipv6.conf.default.forwarding = 1
root@mac:~# ip tunnel add tun6to4 mode sit remote any local 81.165.101.125
root@mac:~# ip link set dev tun6to4 mtu 1472 up
root@mac:~# ip link show dev tun6to4
10: tun6to4: <NOARP,UP,LOWER_UP> mtu 1472 qdisc noqueue state UNKNOWN
    link/sit 81.165.101.125 brd 0.0.0.0
root@mac:~# ip -6 addr add dev tun6to4 2002:51a5:657d:0::1/64
root@mac:~# ip -6 addr add dev eth0 2002:51a5:657d:1::1/64
root@mac:~# ip -6 addr add dev eth0 fdcb:43c1:9c18:1::1/64
root@mac:~# ifconfig
eth0        Link encap:Ethernet  HWaddr 00:26:bb:5d:2e:52
            inet addr:81.165.101.125  Bcast:255.255.255.255  Mask:255.255.248.0
            inet6 addr: fe80::226:bbff:fe5d:2e52/64 Scope:Link
            inet6 addr: fdcb:43c1:9c18:1::1/64 Scope:Global
            inet6 addr: 2002:51a5:657d:1::1/64 Scope:Global
            UP BROADCAST RUNNING MULTICAST  MTU:1500  Metric:1
            RX packets:5927436 errors:0 dropped:0 overruns:0 frame:0
            TX packets:2986025 errors:0 dropped:0 overruns:0 carrier:0
            collisions:0 txqueuelen:1000
            RX bytes:4274948430 (4.2 GB)  TX bytes:237014619 (237.0 MB)
            Interrupt:43 Base address:0x8000

lo          Link encap:Local Loopback
            inet addr:127.0.0.1  Mask:255.0.0.0
            inet6 addr: ::1/128 Scope:Host
            UP LOOPBACK RUNNING  MTU:16436  Metric:1
            RX packets:598 errors:0 dropped:0 overruns:0 frame:0
            TX packets:598 errors:0 dropped:0 overruns:0 carrier:0
            collisions:0 txqueuelen:0
            RX bytes:61737 (61.7 KB)  TX bytes:61737 (61.7 KB)

tun6to4     Link encap:IPv6-in-IPv4
            inet6 addr: ::81.165.101.125/128 Scope:Compat
            inet6 addr: 2002:51a5:657d::1/64 Scope:Global
            UP RUNNING NOARP  MTU:1472  Metric:1
            RX packets:0 errors:0 dropped:0 overruns:0 frame:0
            TX packets:0 errors:0 dropped:0 overruns:0 carrier:0
            collisions:0 txqueuelen:0
            RX bytes:0 (0.0 B)  TX bytes:0 (0.0 B)

root@mac:~# ip -6 route add 2002::/16 dev tun6to4
root@mac:~# ip -6 route add ::/0 via ::192.88.99.1 dev tun6to4 metric 1
root@mac:~# ip -6 route show
::/96 via :: dev tun6to4  metric 256  mtu 1472 advmss 1412 hoplimit 0
2002:51a5:657d::/64 dev tun6to4  proto kernel  metric 256  mtu 1472 advmss 1412 hoplimit 0
2002:51a5:657d:1::/64 dev eth0  proto kernel  metric 256  mtu 1500 advmss 1440 hoplimit 0
```

```
2002::/16 dev tun6to4  metric 1024  mtu 1472 advmss 1412 hoplimit 0
fdcb:43c1:9c18:1::/64 dev eth0  proto kernel  metric 256  mtu 1500 advmss 1440 hoplimit 0
fe80::/64 dev eth0  proto kernel  metric 256  mtu 1500 advmss 1440 hoplimit 0
fe80::/64 dev tun6to4  proto kernel  metric 256  mtu 1472 advmss 1412 hoplimit 0
default via ::192.88.99.1 dev tun6to4  metric 1  mtu 1472 advmss 1412 hoplimit 0
root@mac:~# ping6 ipv6-test.com
PING ipv6-test.com(ipv6-test.com) 56 data bytes
64 bytes from ipv6-test.com: icmp_seq=1 ttl=57 time=42.4 ms
64 bytes from ipv6-test.com: icmp_seq=2 ttl=57 time=43.0 ms
64 bytes from ipv6-test.com: icmp_seq=3 ttl=57 time=43.5 ms
64 bytes from ipv6-test.com: icmp_seq=4 ttl=57 time=43.9 ms
64 bytes from ipv6-test.com: icmp_seq=5 ttl=57 time=45.6 ms
^C
--- ipv6-test.com ping statistics ---
5 packets transmitted, 5 received, 0% packet loss, time 4006ms
rtt min/avg/max/mdev = 42.485/43.717/45.632/1.091 ms
```

Part X. Appendices

Table of Contents

Appendix A. cloning

A.1. About cloning

You can have distinct goals for cloning a server. For instance a clone can be a cold iron backup system used for manual disaster recovery of a service. Or a clone can be created to serve in a test environment. Or you might want to make an almost identical server. Let's take a look at some offline and online ways to create a clone of a Linux server.

A.2. About offline cloning

The term offline cloning is used when you power off the running Linux server to create the clone. This method is easy since we don't have to consider open files and we don't have to skip virtual file systems like **/dev** or **/sys** . The offline cloning method can be broken down into these steps:

```
1. Boot source and target server with a bootable CD
2. Partition, format and mount volumes on the target server
3. Copy files/partitions from source to target over the network
```

The first step is trivial. The second step is explained in the Disk Management chapter. For the third step, you can use a combination of **ssh** or **netcat** with **cp**, **dd**, **dump** and **restore**, **tar**, **cpio**, **rsync** or even **cat**.

A.3. Offline cloning example

We have a working Red Hat Enterprise Linux 5 server, and we want a perfect copy of it on newer hardware. First thing to do is discover the disk layout.

```
[root@RHEL5 ~]# df -h
Filesystem        Size  Used Avail Use% Mounted on
/dev/sda2          15G  4.5G  9.3G  33% /
/dev/sda1          99M   31M   64M  33% /boot
```

The **/boot** partition is small but big enough. If we create an identical partition, then **dd** should be a good cloning option. Suppose the / partition needs to be enlarged on the target system. The best option then is to use a combination of **dump** and **restore**. Remember that dd copies blocks, whereas dump/restore copies files.

The first step to do is to boot the target server with a live CD and partition the target disk. To do this we use the Red Hat Enterprise Linux 5 install CD. At the CD boot prompt we type "linux rescue". The cd boots into a root console where we can use fdisk to discover and prepare the attached disks.

When the partitions are created and have their filesystem, then we can use dd to copy the / boot partition.

```
ssh root@192.168.1.40 "dd if=/dev/sda1" | dd of=/dev/sda1
```

Then we use a dump and restore combo to copy the / partition.

```
mkdir /mnt/x
mount /dev/sda2 /mnt/x
cd /mnt/x
ssh root@192.168.1.40 "dump -0 -f - /" | restore -r -f -
```

Appendix B. License

0. PREAMBLE

The purpose of this License is to make a manual, textbook, or other
functional and useful document "free" in the sense of freedom: to
assure everyone the effective freedom to copy and redistribute it,
with or without modifying it, either commercially or noncommercially.
Secondarily, this License preserves for the author and publisher a way
to get credit for their work, while not being considered responsible
for modifications made by others.

This License is a kind of "copyleft", which means that derivative
works of the document must themselves be free in the same sense. It
complements the GNU General Public License, which is a copyleft
license designed for free software.

We have designed this License in order to use it for manuals for free
software, because free software needs free documentation: a free
program should come with manuals providing the same freedoms that the
software does. But this License is not limited to software manuals; it
can be used for any textual work, regardless of subject matter or
whether it is published as a printed book. We recommend this License
principally for works whose purpose is instruction or reference.

1. APPLICABILITY AND DEFINITIONS

This License applies to any manual or other work, in any medium, that
contains a notice placed by the copyright holder saying it can be
distributed under the terms of this License. Such a notice grants a
world-wide, royalty-free license, unlimited in duration, to use that
work under the conditions stated herein. The "Document", below, refers
to any such manual or work. Any member of the public is a licensee,
and is addressed as "you". You accept the license if you copy, modify
or distribute the work in a way requiring permission under copyright
law.

A "Modified Version" of the Document means any work containing the
Document or a portion of it, either copied verbatim, or with
modifications and/or translated into another language.

A "Secondary Section" is a named appendix or a front-matter section of
the Document that deals exclusively with the relationship of the
publishers or authors of the Document to the Document's overall
subject (or to related matters) and contains nothing that could fall
directly within that overall subject. (Thus, if the Document is in
part a textbook of mathematics, a Secondary Section may not explain
any mathematics.) The relationship could be a matter of historical
connection with the subject or with related matters, or of legal,
commercial, philosophical, ethical or political position regarding
them.

The "Invariant Sections" are certain Secondary Sections whose titles are designated, as being those of Invariant Sections, in the notice that says that the Document is released under this License. If a section does not fit the above definition of Secondary then it is not allowed to be designated as Invariant. The Document may contain zero Invariant Sections. If the Document does not identify any Invariant Sections then there are none.

The "Cover Texts" are certain short passages of text that are listed, as Front-Cover Texts or Back-Cover Texts, in the notice that says that the Document is released under this License. A Front-Cover Text may be at most 5 words, and a Back-Cover Text may be at most 25 words.

A "Transparent" copy of the Document means a machine-readable copy, represented in a format whose specification is available to the general public, that is suitable for revising the document straightforwardly with generic text editors or (for images composed of pixels) generic paint programs or (for drawings) some widely available drawing editor, and that is suitable for input to text formatters or for automatic translation to a variety of formats suitable for input to text formatters. A copy made in an otherwise Transparent file format whose markup, or absence of markup, has been arranged to thwart or discourage subsequent modification by readers is not Transparent. An image format is not Transparent if used for any substantial amount of text. A copy that is not "Transparent" is called "Opaque".

Examples of suitable formats for Transparent copies include plain ASCII without markup, Texinfo input format, LaTeX input format, SGML or XML using a publicly available DTD, and standard-conforming simple HTML, PostScript or PDF designed for human modification. Examples of transparent image formats include PNG, XCF and JPG. Opaque formats include proprietary formats that can be read and edited only by proprietary word processors, SGML or XML for which the DTD and/or processing tools are not generally available, and the machine-generated HTML, PostScript or PDF produced by some word processors for output purposes only.

The "Title Page" means, for a printed book, the title page itself, plus such following pages as are needed to hold, legibly, the material this License requires to appear in the title page. For works in formats which do not have any title page as such, "Title Page" means the text near the most prominent appearance of the work's title, preceding the beginning of the body of the text.

The "publisher" means any person or entity that distributes copies of the Document to the public.

A section "Entitled XYZ" means a named subunit of the Document whose title either is precisely XYZ or contains XYZ in parentheses following text that translates XYZ in another language. (Here XYZ stands for a specific section name mentioned below, such as "Acknowledgements", "Dedications", "Endorsements", or "History".) To "Preserve the Title" of such a section when you modify the Document means that it remains a section "Entitled XYZ" according to this definition.

The Document may include Warranty Disclaimers next to the notice which states that this License applies to the Document. These Warranty Disclaimers are considered to be included by reference in this License, but only as regards disclaiming warranties: any other implication that these Warranty Disclaimers may have is void and has no effect on the meaning of this License.

2. VERBATIM COPYING

You may copy and distribute the Document in any medium, either commercially or noncommercially, provided that this License, the copyright notices, and the license notice saying this License applies to the Document are reproduced in all copies, and that you add no other conditions whatsoever to those of this License. You may not use technical measures to obstruct or control the reading or further copying of the copies you make or distribute. However, you may accept compensation in exchange for copies. If you distribute a large enough number of copies you must also follow the conditions in section 3.

You may also lend copies, under the same conditions stated above, and you may publicly display copies.

3. COPYING IN QUANTITY

If you publish printed copies (or copies in media that commonly have printed covers) of the Document, numbering more than 100, and the Document's license notice requires Cover Texts, you must enclose the copies in covers that carry, clearly and legibly, all these Cover Texts: Front-Cover Texts on the front cover, and Back-Cover Texts on the back cover. Both covers must also clearly and legibly identify you as the publisher of these copies. The front cover must present the full title with all words of the title equally prominent and visible. You may add other material on the covers in addition. Copying with changes limited to the covers, as long as they preserve the title of the Document and satisfy these conditions, can be treated as verbatim copying in other respects.

If the required texts for either cover are too voluminous to fit legibly, you should put the first ones listed (as many as fit reasonably) on the actual cover, and continue the rest onto adjacent pages.

If you publish or distribute Opaque copies of the Document numbering more than 100, you must either include a machine-readable Transparent copy along with each Opaque copy, or state in or with each Opaque copy a computer-network location from which the general network-using public has access to download using public-standard network protocols a complete Transparent copy of the Document, free of added material. If you use the latter option, you must take reasonably prudent steps, when you begin distribution of Opaque copies in quantity, to ensure that this Transparent copy will remain thus accessible at the stated location until at least one year after the last time you distribute an Opaque copy (directly or through your agents or retailers) of that edition to the public.

It is requested, but not required, that you contact the authors of the Document well before redistributing any large number of copies, to give them a chance to provide you with an updated version of the Document.

4. MODIFICATIONS

You may copy and distribute a Modified Version of the Document under the conditions of sections 2 and 3 above, provided that you release the Modified Version under precisely this License, with the Modified Version filling the role of the Document, thus licensing distribution and modification of the Modified Version to whoever possesses a copy of it. In addition, you must do these things in the Modified Version:

   * A. Use in the Title Page (and on the covers, if any) a title distinct from that of the Document, and from those of previous versions (which should, if there were any, be listed in the History section of the Document). You may use the same title as a previous version if the original publisher of that version gives permission.

* B. List on the Title Page, as authors, one or more persons or entities responsible for authorship of the modifications in the Modified Version, together with at least five of the principal authors of the Document (all of its principal authors, if it has fewer than five), unless they release you from this requirement.
* C. State on the Title page the name of the publisher of the Modified Version, as the publisher.
* D. Preserve all the copyright notices of the Document.
* E. Add an appropriate copyright notice for your modifications adjacent to the other copyright notices.
* F. Include, immediately after the copyright notices, a license notice giving the public permission to use the Modified Version under the terms of this License, in the form shown in the Addendum below.
* G. Preserve in that license notice the full lists of Invariant Sections and required Cover Texts given in the Document's license notice.
* H. Include an unaltered copy of this License.
* I. Preserve the section Entitled "History", Preserve its Title, and add to it an item stating at least the title, year, new authors, and publisher of the Modified Version as given on the Title Page. If there is no section Entitled "History" in the Document, create one stating the title, year, authors, and publisher of the Document as given on its Title Page, then add an item describing the Modified Version as stated in the previous sentence.
* J. Preserve the network location, if any, given in the Document for public access to a Transparent copy of the Document, and likewise the network locations given in the Document for previous versions it was based on. These may be placed in the "History" section. You may omit a network location for a work that was published at least four years before the Document itself, or if the original publisher of the version it refers to gives permission.
* K. For any section Entitled "Acknowledgements" or "Dedications", Preserve the Title of the section, and preserve in the section all the substance and tone of each of the contributor acknowledgements and/or dedications given therein.
* L. Preserve all the Invariant Sections of the Document, unaltered in their text and in their titles. Section numbers or the equivalent are not considered part of the section titles.
* M. Delete any section Entitled "Endorsements". Such a section may not be included in the Modified Version.
* N. Do not retitle any existing section to be Entitled "Endorsements" or to conflict in title with any Invariant Section.
* O. Preserve any Warranty Disclaimers.

If the Modified Version includes new front-matter sections or appendices that qualify as Secondary Sections and contain no material copied from the Document, you may at your option designate some or all of these sections as invariant. To do this, add their titles to the list of Invariant Sections in the Modified Version's license notice. These titles must be distinct from any other section titles.

You may add a section Entitled "Endorsements", provided it contains nothing but endorsements of your Modified Version by various parties—for example, statements of peer review or that the text has been approved by an organization as the authoritative definition of a standard.

You may add a passage of up to five words as a Front-Cover Text, and a passage of up to 25 words as a Back-Cover Text, to the end of the list of Cover Texts in the Modified Version. Only one passage of Front-Cover Text and one of Back-Cover Text may be added by (or through arrangements made by) any one entity. If the Document already includes a cover text for the same cover, previously added by you or by arrangement made by the same entity you are acting on behalf of, you may not add another; but you may replace the old one, on explicit permission from the previous publisher that added the old one.

The author(s) and publisher(s) of the Document do not by this License give permission to use their names for publicity for or to assert or imply endorsement of any Modified Version.

5. COMBINING DOCUMENTS

You may combine the Document with other documents released under this License, under the terms defined in section 4 above for modified versions, provided that you include in the combination all of the Invariant Sections of all of the original documents, unmodified, and list them all as Invariant Sections of your combined work in its license notice, and that you preserve all their Warranty Disclaimers.

The combined work need only contain one copy of this License, and multiple identical Invariant Sections may be replaced with a single copy. If there are multiple Invariant Sections with the same name but different contents, make the title of each such section unique by adding at the end of it, in parentheses, the name of the original author or publisher of that section if known, or else a unique number. Make the same adjustment to the section titles in the list of Invariant Sections in the license notice of the combined work.

In the combination, you must combine any sections Entitled "History" in the various original documents, forming one section Entitled "History"; likewise combine any sections Entitled "Acknowledgements", and any sections Entitled "Dedications". You must delete all sections Entitled "Endorsements".

6. COLLECTIONS OF DOCUMENTS

You may make a collection consisting of the Document and other documents released under this License, and replace the individual copies of this License in the various documents with a single copy that is included in the collection, provided that you follow the rules of this License for verbatim copying of each of the documents in all other respects.

You may extract a single document from such a collection, and distribute it individually under this License, provided you insert a copy of this License into the extracted document, and follow this License in all other respects regarding verbatim copying of that document.

7. AGGREGATION WITH INDEPENDENT WORKS

A compilation of the Document or its derivatives with other separate and independent documents or works, in or on a volume of a storage or distribution medium, is called an "aggregate" if the copyright resulting from the compilation is not used to limit the legal rights of the compilation's users beyond what the individual works permit. When the Document is included in an aggregate, this License does not apply to the other works in the aggregate which are not themselves derivative works of the Document.

If the Cover Text requirement of section 3 is applicable to these copies of the Document, then if the Document is less than one half of the entire aggregate, the Document's Cover Texts may be placed on covers that bracket the Document within the aggregate, or the electronic equivalent of covers if the Document is in electronic form. Otherwise they must appear on printed covers that bracket the whole aggregate.

8. TRANSLATION

Translation is considered a kind of modification, so you may distribute translations of the Document under the terms of section 4. Replacing Invariant Sections with translations requires special permission from their copyright holders, but you may include translations of some or all Invariant Sections in addition to the original versions of these Invariant Sections. You may include a translation of this License, and all the license notices in the Document, and any Warranty Disclaimers, provided that you also include the original English version of this License and the original versions of those notices and disclaimers. In case of a disagreement between the translation and the original version of this License or a notice or disclaimer, the original version will prevail.

If a section in the Document is Entitled "Acknowledgements", "Dedications", or "History", the requirement (section 4) to Preserve its Title (section 1) will typically require changing the actual title.

9. TERMINATION

You may not copy, modify, sublicense, or distribute the Document except as expressly provided under this License. Any attempt otherwise to copy, modify, sublicense, or distribute it is void, and will automatically terminate your rights under this License.

However, if you cease all violation of this License, then your license from a particular copyright holder is reinstated (a) provisionally, unless and until the copyright holder explicitly and finally terminates your license, and (b) permanently, if the copyright holder fails to notify you of the violation by some reasonable means prior to 60 days after the cessation.

Moreover, your license from a particular copyright holder is reinstated permanently if the copyright holder notifies you of the violation by some reasonable means, this is the first time you have received notice of violation of this License (for any work) from that copyright holder, and you cure the violation prior to 30 days after your receipt of the notice.

Termination of your rights under this section does not terminate the licenses of parties who have received copies or rights from you under this License. If your rights have been terminated and not permanently reinstated, receipt of a copy of some or all of the same material does not give you any rights to use it.

10. FUTURE REVISIONS OF THIS LICENSE

The Free Software Foundation may publish new, revised versions of the GNU Free Documentation License from time to time. Such new versions will be similar in spirit to the present version, but may differ in detail to address new problems or concerns. See http://www.gnu.org/copyleft/.

Each version of the License is given a distinguishing version number. If the Document specifies that a particular numbered version of this License "or any later version" applies to it, you have the option of following the terms and conditions either of that specified version or of any later version that has been published (not as a draft) by the Free Software Foundation. If the Document does not specify a version number of this License, you may choose any version ever published (not as a draft) by the Free Software Foundation. If the Document specifies that a proxy can decide which future versions of this License can be used, that proxy's public statement of acceptance of a version permanently authorizes you to choose that version for the Document.

11. RELICENSING

"Massive Multiauthor Collaboration Site" (or "MMC Site") means any World Wide Web server that publishes copyrightable works and also provides prominent facilities for anybody to edit those works. A public wiki that anybody can edit is an example of such a server. A "Massive Multiauthor Collaboration" (or "MMC") contained in the site means any set of copyrightable works thus published on the MMC site.

"CC-BY-SA" means the Creative Commons Attribution-Share Alike 3.0 license published by Creative Commons Corporation, a not-for-profit corporation with a principal place of business in San Francisco, California, as well as future copyleft versions of that license published by that same organization.

"Incorporate" means to publish or republish a Document, in whole or in part, as part of another Document.

An MMC is "eligible for relicensing" if it is licensed under this License, and if all works that were first published under this License somewhere other than this MMC, and subsequently incorporated in whole or in part into the MMC, (1) had no cover texts or invariant sections, and (2) were thus incorporated prior to November 1, 2008.

The operator of an MMC Site may republish an MMC contained in the site under CC-BY-SA on the same site at any time before August 1, 2009, provided the MMC is eligible for relicensing.

Index

Symbols

/etc/apache2, 10
/etc/bind/named.conf.local, 76
/etc/group, 45
/etc/httpd, 10
/etc/inetd.conf, 152
/etc/init.d/samba, 141
/etc/init.d/smb, 141
/etc/init.d/winbind, 142
/etc/nsswitch.conf, 190, 192
/etc/passwd, 45, 199
/etc/resolv.conf, 62
/etc/samba/passdb.tdb, 198
/etc/samba/smb.conf, 146, 147, 148, 164, 188
/etc/samba/smbpasswd, 169, 196
/etc/selinux/config, 212
/etc/squid/squid.conf, 34
/etc/sysctl.conf, 116
/etc/xinetd.d/swat, 152
/proc/sys/net/ipv4/ip_forward, 116
/selinux, 214
/selinux/enforce, 214
/var/log/audit/audit.log, 210
/var/log/squid, 39
.htaccess, 27
.htpasswd, 17, 24
.my.cnf, 46

A

A (DNS record), 67
AAAA (DNS record), 67
allow hosts (Samba), 181
apache2, 6
aptitude, 138, 139, 227
aptitude(8), 44
auditd, 210
authoritative (dns), 71
authoritative zone, 66
axfr, 74

B

bind, 64
bind(DNS), 90
browsable (Samba), 182
browseable (Samba), 182
browser master, 196

C

cahing only name server, 68
chain (iptables), 123
char(mysql), 49
chcon(1), 216, 217
chkconfig, 210
chmod, 213

CIFS, 143
CNAME (DNS record), 67
context type(selinux), 215
create(mysql), 47, 49, 55
create mask (Samba), 182

D

delete(mysql), 54
deny hosts (Samba), 182
describe(mysql), 50
dhclient, 118
dhcp server, 62
directory mask (Samba), 182
directory security mask(samba), 183
DNAT, 115
dns, 60, 60
dnsdomainname, 66
dns namespace, 63
dns server, 62
domain (dns), 64
domain name system, 60, 60
dpkg, 138
dpkg(1), 44
drop(mysql), 48, 50, 56

F

filter table (iptables), 123
firewall, 114
force create mode(samba), 183
force directory mode(samba), 183
force directory security mode(samba), 183
force group(samba), 170
force security mode(samba), 183
force user(samba), 170
forwarder (dns), 70
forward lookup query, 61
fqdn, 66
fully qualified domain name, 66

G

getenforce, 211
getent(1), 191
getfattr(1), 217
git, 226
github, 232
glue record (dns), 67
grant(mysql), 48
group by(mysql), 54
guest ok (Samba), 157

H

hide unreadable (Samba), 182
host (DNS record), 67
hostname, 66, 143
hosts.txt, 60
hosts allow (Samba), 181
hosts deny (Samba), 182

smbtree(1), 150
smtp, 67
SNAT, 115
soa (dns record), 71
SQL, 43, 51
squid, 33
stateful firewall, 114
swat(8), 152
sysctl, 116

T

tcpdump, 61, 118
tdbsam, 170, 196, 198
testparm(1), 147, 147, 148
tld, 65
TLD (dns), 65
top level domain, 65
transition(selinux), 216
trigger(mysql), 55
triggers(mysql), 44
type(selinux), 215

U

update(mysql), 52
use(mysql), 48

V

valid users (Samba), 181
varchar(mysql), 49
virtualbox, 117
vmware, 117

W

wbinfo(1), 190, 191
webalizer, 27
winbind(8), 190
winbind(samba), 188
winbindd(8), 142, 142, 190
wireshark, 118
workgroup, 157
writable (Samba), 164
write list (Samba), 181

X

xinetd(8), 152

Y

yum, 139

Z

zone (dns), 66, 71
zone transfer (dns), 71

www.ingramcontent.com/pod-product-compliance
Lightning Source LLC
LaVergne TN
LVHW060138070326
832902LV00018B/2843